I'm Speaking Up but You're Not Listening!

Second Edition

Charlena E. Jackson, B.S., M.S., M.H.A

Cover design by Annabelle Pullen Instagram username (@artofannabellepullen) artofannabellepullen@gmail.com
Formatting by Polgarus Studio

Printed in the United States of America
2nd edition, October 2019
ISBN: 978-1-7335666-8-1 (print)
ISBN: 978-1-7335666-9-8 (ebook)

BOOKS BY CHARLENA E. JACKSON, B.S., M.S., M.H.A

No Cross, No Crown: Trust God Through the Battle
No Cross, No Crown: Trust God Through the Battle 2nd edition
I'm Speaking Up but You're Not Listening
I'm Speaking Up but You're Not Listening 2nd edition
Teachers Just Don't Understand Bullying Hurts
Teachers Just Don't Understand Bullying Hurts 2nd edition
A Woman's Love is Never Good Enough
A Woman's Love is Never Good Enough 2nd Edition
Unapologetic for My Flaws and All
Unapologetic for My Flaws and All 2nd edition
Dying on the Inside and Suffocating on the Outside
Dear Fathers of the Fatherless Children

To my beloved son, Elijah and my niece Charrese – always remember, fear cannot be your leader. Most importantly, remember your voice matters. Daddy, thank you for your unconditional love and for always teaching my siblings and me not to be afraid to speak and stand up for what we believe in.

Contents

Introduction 1

1. The Silent Killer...3

2. Forms of Bullying 6

3. Silence is not Golden 16

4. What's Wrong with Me?..28

5. Our Children's Voices Matter.....................................39

6. Enough is Enough 48

7. Higher Authority 58

8. Take Time to Listen...70

9. What About Us? 79

10. Understanding the Message 91

11. Atlanta Neighborhood Charter School (ANCS) Journey....................99

About the Author..129

Introduction

WE WANT TO PROTECT our children by any means necessary. Sadly, we cannot be with them every moment of the day. I never thought I would have to teach my children to defend themselves at such a young age. Children are supposed to be free spirits, dream chasers, and thinking of limitless opportunities. They are supposed to be filled with light that shines with happiness and joy that shouldn't be dimmed or filled with darkness and fear.

Children should be living carefree lives and always smiling, laughing, filled with peace, and harmony; not worrying about the troubles of what tomorrow may bring. Our children should have a wide range of imagination and think about the greatest achievements that they want to accomplish; not making sacrifices by having to give up their clothes, lunch money, or being robbed of their personality, and stripped of their self-esteem.

As parents, guardians, teachers, and school administrators, we should be giving our children better days, we are the outcome of their future, we are the pieces of the puzzle – pieces that restore their shattered confidence. When our children are hopeless, we are the light that shines brightly to renew their hope. Our love and actions are the hope that floats to restore what was lost and to renew strength that they never imagined existed.

We are our children's voices when all else has failed. As parents, guardians, teachers, and school administrators, we have to be more involved in our children's lives. Bullying shouldn't be taken lightly. However, it's a sad fact that bullying is played down in schools by some teachers, administrators, and sometimes at home by the parents.

We have to change this continuous cycle. It has gone on too far for way too long. Our children shouldn't be victims of suicide or have suicidal thoughts because someone thinks they have the ability to strip them bit by bit and piece by piece of their birthright of life.

We must fight for our children; our voices are louder and the roar of our demand for change will be heard loud and clear. We will burn the ashes of fear from our children because we are a source of empowerment.

Our children are special, they are unique, they are a gift, and they are our children that we love dearly. Without a doubt, change will come and we must make that change happen because bullying is not accepted.

We shouldn't give anyone the ability to rob our children of happiness. We have the power to change the situation. For those who feel as though bullying is an unknown situation, let's dare to be different and make the situation known by opening the problem at hand by speaking up and finding a solution to the problem. We should always remember, when a problem occurs, we must not forget that there's always a solution.

Now is the time to decide to make the change. Now is the time to dissect and look at every angle in the distasteful world of bullying. Now is the time for us to put our best foot forward and take on the responsibility of saving our children from being killed or destroyed by bullying; also, known as the Silent Killer. Our children shouldn't be prisoners of what a bully has cast on them. Our children want their voices to be heard; and as the adults in charge, our voices deserve to be heard.

The time has come to take action to stop bullying – and the time is now!

CHAPTER 1

The Silent Killer

NOBODY IS PERFECT; HOWEVER, some people act as though we live in a perfect world. I can never understand why people judge one another by their clothes, race, gender, religion, or for their own selfish reasons. Bullying is a silent killer because it is truly ignored and goes unnoticed.

Our children shouldn't have to feel they have to face this battle on their own. They shouldn't have to second guess if they have to fight their battles alone. Our children are fighting a silent war because they are broken down and tired. They isolate themselves from the pain. Deep inside they are screaming for help. They should not fight this silent killer alone.

As parents, guardians, teachers, school administrators, and higher authorities, we should break the tension, break the pattern of helplessness, hopelessness, and break the battle they are fighting with themselves.

Our children need us but the silent killer keeps them isolated. It keeps their mind roaming on the "What if's", "Why me", "Should I?" and so much more.

The silent killer puts pressure on our children to be perfect – as if they don't have any flaws. It changes their identity to the point that we do not know who our children have become. It changes our children and leads them into a shadowy place, which sometimes is a road that has no return. That road is a never-ending road of darkness. The silent killer's home is a dark place and it swallows our children by taking them deeper into a dungeon of lies. It has control over our children's minds, and our children start to think they are not good enough. They go deeper into the dark place and begin to hurt themselves, and shut themselves off from the rest of the world.

The silent killer takes hold of our children to make them feel unworthy, to the point that the child we once knew who was so loving, kind, happy, always smiling, and filled with joy is now depressed and shattered into a trillion pieces, and who has suicidal thoughts.

The silent killer does not weep over our children; instead, it sucks the life out of them until it has fully destroyed our children with the burden of stress and worries. This is what a child should not have to endure.

The silent killer ties our children's tongues to the extent that our children do not seek help. It numbs our children's minds to only think negative thoughts. The silent killer hypnotizes their lives to the point that our children cannot recognize themselves anymore. The darkness of the silent killer pushes our children to their breaking point, and sometimes to the point of death.

Our children shouldn't live in darkness. Our children shouldn't feel alone. The silent killer does not have the right to suffocate our children and take their souls. We, as the parents, guardians, teachers, school administrators, and higher authorities have to take a stand and confront the silent killer. Our children shouldn't suffer or be in despair on a daily basis.

The silent killer has our children running mentally and physically day and night. From scarring them with their words during the day to leaving a mental scar on them each night, and preventing them from a peaceful night's rest.

When our children are standing in one place they are still running on the inside, filled with torture, misery, and thinking over and over again that there's no way out.

Our children begin to drift away because of the scars and burdens. The sharp tongue of the silent killer constantly creates a cloud of confusion and friction over our children's heads due to the verbal, mental, emotional, and physical abuse.

We do not want our children to fade into the background and have a mental breakdown. We have to catch them before they fall; if not, there's a possibility that they will be in danger of having a mental disturbance disorder due to the pressure, stress, depression, and pain they have endured for such a long time.

The silent killer distracts our children from their studies and constantly traumatizes them. It steals their joy and it intimidates their train of thought. The darkness of the silent killer plays mind games with our children. It makes them doubt their ability to ask for help. It makes them slip further down, drowning deeper and deeper in doubt. Our children then begin to think they do not know who to trust; they build up a wall and let themselves go, they give in and become a prisoner of the silent killer.

We have to save our children. We have to break down our children's walls patiently with the understanding that they will come around slowly but surely. The silent killer of darkness will not win. We have to bring the light out of our brittle and fragile children.

We cannot let our children's lives pass them by. Although they might think they've hit a low point, we have to be the ones to revive our children and bring them back to life; to hit an all-time high. We must let them know they are not defective or destroyed; instead, they are brave for having the courage to talk to someone, seek help, and trust again; and we need to reassure our children that it is not their fault.

As parents, guardians, teachers, school administrators, and higher authorities, we have to break the silent killer by all means necessary. If not, the darkness of the silent killer will lead our children down the path of isolation, fear, and possibly to a path of death.

CHAPTER 2

Forms of Bullying

DON'T BE FOOLED BY what you see. Bullying comes in all sizes, shapes, genders, races, religions, and ages. Verbal threats, stealing, intimidation, exclusion, physical harm, name-calling, humiliation, and manipulations are some tactics that are serious — and forms of bullying.

Bullying doesn't just consist of students bullying one another. I have seen children being bullied by their parents, guardians, teachers/educators, and higher authorities. What does that achieve?

Honestly, it is really sad. I think to myself, who are children supposed to trust? Who are they supposed to confide in if the "adults" are the ones who are the bullies? When a child is bullied by an adult how should a child respond? The child cannot fight back or take up for themselves when it comes to confronting an adult that is the bully.

When a child is being bullied by a grown-up it changes their frame of thinking, and at times they shut down because they feel confined in a box with no one to turn to. Some children hesitate to speak to their parents or a responsible adult because they feel an adult would believe the other adult over a child.

When I was in sixth grade, my teacher told my father I had disrespected him, which wasn't true. The teacher was very upset because he asked me to wash the board and clean the band room as punishment for something I did not do. As I was sitting down in the band room, one of my classmates scooted my chair back without my knowing. I neglected to look to see if the chair was there before I sat down; because it had been there when I got up to adjust my stand and music sheet. After I cleaned my clarinet I "thought" I was going to sit in my chair; instead, I landed right on a hard tile floor. I knew who did it, because once before the girl stole my clarinet and lied about it.

After I fell on the floor the entire class was laughing. It was humiliating. The band teacher was outside talking to another teacher. I jumped up and punched the girl in the face. I was sick of her always picking on me and stealing from me. I'd had enough!

The teacher only saw me defending myself, yet he accused me of starting the fight without bothering to ask what happened. He sent me to the principal's office. However, the girl stayed in class.

I tried explaining to him what happened, but he began to yell at me, saying, "Go to the main office now!" After I went to the main office, I was told I was going to have In-School Suspension (ISS) for a week. The administrator sent me to class with a pass. My teacher told me I had to wash the boards and clean the band room. I told him, no, because I didn't do anything wrong.

He took two steps towards me, got in my face, tightened his lips and said in a firm harsh voice, "You are going to do what I say, or else." I told him, "I catch the school bus home, and I can't miss it." He said, "I don't give a damn how you get home. I do know you are going to do what I say. If not, I will make sure you do not play an instrument for the entire year; and you will clean the band room while you are in class and all the instruments." I looked at him and said, "No."

He yelled at the top of his lungs and said, "Get out of my classroom right now!" As I tried to get my backpack he yelled and said, "This is my classroom! If your stuff is in my classroom it belongs to me, now get out!" I waited outside his classroom until the bell rang. I tried walking in to get my backpack, but he stood in the doorway and wouldn't let me in. I got on the bus without my belongings.

My daddy was home early from work. He asked me how was my day, I told him what happened. He said, "Baby girl, you know there are always three sides to a story; your side, their side, and the truth." He said, "I am going to give you the benefit of the doubt, and after I talk to your teacher, I will make a decision if you are going to be on punishment or not."

Daddy and I went up to the school and we had a teacher, student, and parent conference about the issue. That was the first time in a long time I saw my daddy so upset. The night before, I think he was trying to keep his composure. However, in the meeting, my daddy told my teacher off in a respectful manner, because he wasn't happy with how I was being treated or how my teacher spoke to me.

He spoke with the administrator and principal; he told them they should be aware of how the students were being treated. The administrator acted as if she didn't have a clue what my daddy was talking about. The band teacher told my daddy I was disrespectful and disturbing the class.

My daddy went on and asked, "Did you attempt to listen to her side of the story?" Everyone was silent. My daddy answered the question for them and said, "No, you didn't even think to ask. Furthermore, you didn't think to listen when my daughter tried explaining what happened."

The assistant principal said, "Children are prone to lie to get themselves out of trouble." My daddy said, "How would you know if you didn't take time to listen?" My daddy went on to say, "In my house, my children are able to speak their minds in a respectful way, and I teach my children that in order to receive respect, you have to earn respect, despite your age, because everyone should be treated fairly." (My daddy is a Marine and we had rules and regulations to follow. With that being said, we were raised differently from other children my age, something which I appreciate until this day).

My daddy told me to go to class so he could talk to my teacher, the administrator, and principal alone. I do not know what was said but I do know that I did not have In-School Suspension. The faculty and staff treated me with respect (even teachers whom I didn't know).

When I arrived home my daddy and I had a talk. He explained to me how a human being should be treated. He went into deep detail about how he was proud of me for standing up for myself despite the other person being a higher authority. My daddy took time to talk to me about life and people.

I appreciated my daddy for going to the school to speak on my behalf, and I appreciated my daddy for taking up for me. It made me feel more than loved. It made me feel secure. By my daddy taking time to listen to me, and not believing every word of what the teacher said it gave me a voice and the confidence to speak up. It formed a bond between my daddy and me because I knew I could talk to him about anything without being blamed for something I didn't do.

Sometimes I wonder, what if my daddy didn't listen to me? What if my daddy believed the teachers? What would my life be like today?

If I knew then what I know now, I would have known that I was a student being bullied by my teacher by him threatening me, scolding me, and holding my belongings without my permission.

Teachers bullying students is a topic that is rarely discussed; it's often too complex to identify and to address because of the lies that are being covered up by some of the teachers and administration. They try to make it difficult for parents to defend their children by making up senseless excuses; and/or by trying to convince the student it was their fault. Being bullied by a teacher or administrator in the school system is ignored and not called out for what it is—bullying.

The teachers and administration are bold enough to bully parents as well. They try to convince the parents that something is wrong with their child. They run different tests, monitor the child's behavior, and makeup excuses to make the parent think their child needs special attention and medication to be able to be "tolerated."

Brice, the son of my friend was in seventh grade. He told his mother that he didn't like going to school because his teacher was mean, rude, always embarrassing the students in class by calling him and his classmates names. Jaya admitted that she didn't take what her child said seriously because she thought that he was making up excuses to get out of going to school.

One day, on the way to school, Brice voiced his opinion again and said, "Mom, please do not make me walk into the school building. Please." Jaya parked the car and had a little chat with him. Brice said, "My teacher called me an idiot the other day. Not to mention, she was writing on the board talking to herself out loud saying, "These kids are so dumb I do not know why I am here."

He went on to say, "Mom, she said that because sometimes we do not understand the work and we ask her to repeat herself so we can write down the notes. She says no. We are not supposed to take notes while she's lecturing."

He continued, "Mom, I know we are not supposed to take notes in class, but how can I remember my math equations and how to solve the problem? Then she always making sarcastic remarks and has a nasty spooky smile on her face, saying, "Come on, you guys, I know some of your parents have smart kids." Or she'll say, "I know you better than this, I know at least one of you knows the answer to this kindergarten question; or do I have to walk down the street to get a preschooler to answer this question?"

Brice continued and said, "Mom, one day, she started speaking another language out of nowhere. She was speaking Portuguese and she said to the class, "Why are you guys looking at me with a stupid face? You act like you cannot understand English so I am going to speak another language. Maybe you will understand that." Brice kept talking, "Mom, she spoke Portuguese for the entire session. Not to mention, we had a test the next day, which everyone failed because the day before we were supposed to have a review."

Jaya asked Brice, "Why can't you take notes in math class? That is ridiculously crazy." She was very upset about what her son was saying. Brice said, "Mom, she doesn't like for anyone to write while she's lecturing. She wants to make sure she has everyone's undivided attention." Jaya said, "Okay, but again, that's math. In order to learn you have to practice the problems, and in order to do that you have to take notes. No wonder you are failing math."

Jaya told Brice she would schedule a conference to speak with his teacher.

During the conference, his teacher did not deny what Brice had said. She admitted she did not want her students to take notes in class. Jaya asked the teacher, "Why? In order to learn, you need to take notes." The teacher interrupted Jaya and said in a firm voice, "That might be true, but those are the rules in my class." Jaya said, "Is that so? We will see what we are going to do about changing your rules to the point that they will make sense, as opposed to hindering the students from learning."

The teacher cut her off in a disrespectful way and said, "Is there anything else I can help you with?" Jaya answered, "I'm glad you asked. Why are you speaking another language in class, knowing the students do not understand?" The teacher laughed as if it was funny and replied, "Quite frankly, apparently, they do not understand English, either." Jaya looked at her with a straight face and said, "So you think it's funny? Don't you know you are playing games with the students and their education?" The teacher didn't answer the question. Instead, she told Jaya that the conference had run its course, and to enjoy the rest of her day.

When Jaya reported her to the headteacher of the department, her concerns weren't addressed. She then spoke with the assistant principal, and again her concerns fell on deaf ears. She had a hard time getting in touch with the principal. However, about a month later the principal finally responded by email and ask for a parent, teacher, and principal conference.

During the conference, the teacher had a manila folder filled with documents. Both the teacher and principal expressed their concerns about Brice; they felt as though he had a learning disability. They said they had run numerous tests and they suggested that Brice needed to be seen by a psychiatrist because his behavior in class was unacceptable.

Jaya was filled with indescribable anger. The teacher didn't produce any documents during their conference. She was never told her son had a test performed regarding his learning ability and behavior. As a matter of fact, Brice didn't have a learning disability or behavioral problem. However, Jaya treated them with respect. She addressed the situation and stood firm with the teacher and principal.

Jaya felt she was being bullied. The principal said, "If Brice doesn't see a psychiatrist, I will fill out the documents for the district to approve a school psychiatrist for Brice's needs." Jaya felt like she was being backed into a corner; she told them they were trying to cover up for the teacher's unprofessional behavior — behavior that was never addressed in the conference.

The principal told Jaya that wasn't important, and what was important was Brice's mental ability which was a hazard to the students on the property.

Jaya contacted all the seventh-grade parents in the school directory; they met at a nearby coffee shop and talked about any issues they were having at the school. Some of the parents agreed that their children came home complaining about the same teacher Brice complained about. Some of the parents said they had made complaints about the principal and her behavior. There were parents who made a complaint about their children's safety because the teachers were bullying the students and the parents to a certain extent.

Jaya and the parents gathered together to file a complaint with the Board of Education. In the meantime, Jaya took Brice to see a private psychiatrist. She told the psychiatrist about the situation. The psychiatrist was more than happy to evaluate Brice. She ran every test on Brice that Jaya's insurance would allow. When the tests came back, they determined that Brice was a normal child (which Jaya already knew) and also determined that Brice was a gifted student.

Jaya and the other parents/guardians followed the chain of command with their complaints, but they were ignored by the District and the Board of Education. They tried contacting the local news station but they were told the station wasn't going to get involved with the school system.

Jaya and the parents continued to follow through with their complaints to the Board and principal. Sadly, the only change that was made was the teacher's position. Instead of lecturing in the classroom she became the coordinator over the school's activities. Not only did she have a promotion, but she had a higher salary as well.

What are the parents/guardians to do when some teachers hate their job and are bullying our children? What are the parents/guardians to do when they follow the chain of command yet the administrators of the school system fail to comply with the policies of the District of the State and

Federal Guidelines? What are they supposed to do when the parents and students are being bullied by the educators and administrators?

First, the parents/guardians cannot be afraid to fight for what is right. Justice will be served for our children, and for us as parents. Parents/guardians should always let their primary physician know what is going on so that they will have proof and binding legal documents.

Take to heart what the educators advise you to do regarding the care of your children, especially when they take it to another level as they did with Jaya, by suggesting Brice needed to see a psychiatrist in order to cover up the teacher's wrongdoing. Beat them to the punch, gather your documents, because who knows what they are capable of if they examine your children without your permission? Even if they have your permission, if they feel like you are "stirring up trouble" they could tamper with the exam.

Listen to your children, and even if it sounds like they are telling a fib take note; talk to the teacher about it to nip it in the bud on day one, because what may sound like a fib might be the truth.

Take your addressed concerns to social media. More than likely, you will have a network of parents responding and coming together talking about their situation. By everyone telling their story, this will cause a movement for change.

Seek the advice of an attorney. Sometimes there is only so much a parent/guardian can do, but we can begin by doing things the right way. By taking advantage of our rights we know we have the privilege and freedom to seek a lawyer to fight on our behalf.

My sister was in the middle of her twelfth-grade year when she was jumped by ten girls in the cafeteria. My sister defended herself by throwing chairs to get the girls away from her. When an officer broke up the fight, he tried arresting my sister. He stated that she'd put people's lives in danger by throwing chairs.

When my daddy arrived at the school my sister was in handcuffs. The officer told my dad that he would have to pick my sister up from the police station. My daddy told the officer if he took my sister to the station, he would slap a lawsuit on the school, the county, and him. The officer took the cuffs off my sister, but the situation was far from over.

My daddy spoke to the principal, which wasn't any help. He suspended my sister from school for weeks. Within those weeks, my parents received a letter in the mail stating my sister was kicked out of the school district.

My daddy took the district to court because he knew my sister was treated unfairly. The judge did not rule in my sister's favor. She was kicked out of the school district because one of the girls who jumped her was pregnant, and my sister hit her with an object.

My daddy, asked the judge, "How was my daughter supposed to know the young lady was pregnant? Not only that, why was the young lady jumping my daughter if she knew she was pregnant?"

My daddy went on to say, "How was my daughter supposed to defend herself?" He respectfully reminded the judge that his daughter was jumped by ten girls. Ten girls on one; again, how else was she supposed to defend herself? My daddy asked the judge, "Would it have been better if she was beaten to death and died?"

The judge told my daddy my sister's conduct wasn't acceptable on the school property and that my sister put people's lives in danger and, last but not least, she hit a pregnant young lady.

My daddy asked, "How is my daughter supposed to graduate?"

The judge told my daddy, "That isn't my concern, and as a parent, you need to figure it out."

My daddy didn't give up the fight, he appealed the case because he wasn't going to accept no as the final answer.

A month later, my dad stood forth in front of the same judge. The judge said, "Mr. Jackson, I see you are persistent." My dad replied "Yes, I am. I am my daughter's voice. My daughter wants to be heard. She deserves to be heard. She deserves justice, and I am not going to stop until she receives it."

The judge said, "Mr. Jackson, I have three daughters and if they were jumped by ten people I would not be as humbled as you. I am not making up an excuse for your daughter, but I asked myself the other day, what could she have done differently to defend herself? I couldn't come up with an answer. I asked my daughters if they were jumped by ten people, what would they do?

They said they would pick up anything they could reach to defend themselves."

The judge continued, "I wasn't in your daughter's situation, therefore I can't imagine how she felt, but one thing I do know, if she was my daughter, I would want her to fight for her life. Mr. Jackson, I want to apologize for my actions and words. I grant that your daughter is placed in another district to finish school."

My sister had to stay with my grandmother for the remainder of the year to complete school. My sister didn't march at graduation with her class, but she did graduate high school after taking summer courses.

If my dad hadn't been my sister's voice or put up a fight for my sister, she wouldn't have graduated.

We have to put an end to bullying, whether it's by another student, parent/guardian or an educator. They should be held responsible for their actions.

CHAPTER 3

Silence is not Golden

THERE ARE MANY DEFINITIONS of the word, silence. One could say, Silence is golden. In certain cases, it is, but in a situation when a child is being bullied, silence is the scariest and darkest place to be.

When a child is being bullied, the silence is stealing their soul and sucking the life out of them every single day. They are living in a miserable nightmare day in and out; and on the surface, they are giving a silent cry for help.

Silence goes deep and penetrates the subconscious mind, which influences a person's actions and feelings. Most of the time, when a person dreams, the dreams come from the subconscious mind, because that is where our innermost thoughts lie.

When my son was in kindergarten, I didn't know he was being bullied. He never told me someone was picking on him on a daily basis. I noticed my son's mood started to change, and he always had bad dreams. Not only did he have bad dreams, but he also started to talk out loud while he was dreaming.

He would toss and turn, and at times he would ball up his fist, screaming, "Leave me alone, stop messing with me, why are you doing this to me, stop talking to me, stop it, stop it!" Sometimes I would catch him fighting in his dreams as if he was defending himself and trying to get away.

One day, while he was dreaming, I didn't wake him, I decided to ask him questions. I asked him, "Who's bothering you?" He called out the little boy's name. I asked, "What is he doing?" He told me, "He is calling me names, picking on me, and hitting me for no reason." I then asked, "Did you tell your teachers?" He replied, "Yes, but they do not believe me." The last thing I asked him before I woke him up was, "How long has this been going on?" He said, "For too long, and I am tired of it."

I called my son's name and tapped him softly until he opened his eyes. I said, "Elijah, what were you dreaming about?" He said, "I dreamt of Vince messing with me again. He messes with me at school and in my dreams. I never get a break."

I asked, "Elijah, do you remember me asking you some questions?" He answered, "No."

I then asked, "Elijah, why did you never tell me about it?" He replied, "I didn't think it was a big deal and I thought he would stop picking on me by now."

I told Elijah to never hold anything from me because I need to know so I can help him and put an end to the problem right away. I said, "Elijah if you don't tell me, it will become worse and worse."

Our children are too young to have "real" scary thoughts deep in their minds. Those thoughts could soon be sent to the conscious mind which could then turn into something destructive.

Elijah never had an issue telling me what was going on at school. He would tell me when someone was picking on him or if he felt like he was being mistreated by his peers. I thought that the bullying had silenced his voice until Elijah said softly, "Mom, I think I am being bullied."

I didn't think my son knew what bullying was at such a young age. I asked him, "Why do you feel this way?" He replied, "Every time, I walk into the classroom this little boy always hits me for no reason and he is very mean to me. He takes my pencils and breaks them. He takes all my markers and writes on my paper. During recess, he throws dirt on my clothes for no reason. During lunch, he puts his fingers in my food." He paused and said, "Mom, am I being bullied or is he just picking on me?"

I answered, "Elijah, you are right, you are being bullied."

As Elijah was telling me all that he endured I was thinking to myself, why in the world would a child think of doing such cruel and senseless things? Oh, my goodness, I really believe the child's parent needs to seek professional help for their child.

I had to gather my emotions as Elijah was talking because I was filled with rage, knowing my son was being tortured every single day by this child. I calmly said, "What is your definition of bullying?"

He replied, "When someone is treating you badly. They keep picking on you, hitting, and calling you names after you asked them to leave you alone." I told him, "Yes, that is the right definition for bullying."

The next day, I arrived at the school when his teachers were available to talk. During the conversation, I could tell by their facial expressions that they didn't have a clue about what was going on. After Elijah got his point across and he saw that his teacher and I were concerned, he was more than satisfied and knew the situation was handled.

However, the bullying continued for months. Elijah's spirit changed. When he was at home on the weekend, he would be himself. During the week, he didn't want to go to school, he was always sad and depressed when he got out of school. It was like a dark cloud was following him every day during the week.

I couldn't take any more of him being so young and going through so much at the hands of his classmate. As a parent, I was filled with so much anger, bitterness, and resentment for this little boy, his family, the educators, and the school administrators. I had numerous conversations with the teachers, and nothing changed. I told Elijah, he would have to stand up for himself and start fighting back.

Sure enough, the little boy started to bully Elijah again, and Elijah fought back. Strangely, as Elijah started to fight back, it pissed me off how the teachers only saw when Elijah hit the little boy, but they never saw that the little boy hit Elijah first.

Elijah would come home in a silent state. I would ask Elijah, "What happened today?" I knew it was Vince. Elijah would hold his head down and talk very softly (as if he was thinking it doesn't matter) "Mom, I told my teachers about Vince, but they never do anything about it. They asked us to talk it out. How are we going to do that, Mom? How?"

He began to yell (which wasn't like Elijah to do) "Mom, why do you and everyone else tell me to tell the teachers, and they never do anything about it? Huh? What's the point! I am not telling them anything anymore, because when I do, they never listen, or they roll their eyes as though I am lying, or they tell me to be quiet. Mom, here is the kicker of it all, they tell me they are going to take care of it, but they never do. What am I supposed to do?"

I told Elijah, "I know you do not want to fight back, because two wrongs do not make a right, but you have to start taking up for yourself. In the meantime, I will go back up to the school to talk to the assistant principal and the principal. Trust me, I am going to take care of it."

Every day, Elijah either shut down or was filled with anger. I felt like I'd lost my son due to this little boy bullying him. Silence wasn't golden. I talked to the administrators of the school, yet both of the principals were saying, "I see Elijah talk to Vince all the time and they play during recess."

I was looking at them like, you have got to be kidding me. I told them both, "I can't tell you what you see, but one thing's for sure, I know for a fact, my son is not friends with Vince, so please stop dancing around the problem here." Both of them went on to say, "Well, kids will be kids, they are friends one day, and the next they are upset with each other." I looked at them and told them boldly, "I am not here for you to make up excuses."

Before I finished my sentence, the principal cut me off and said, "Charlena, the little boy that bothers Elijah has a disability but we cannot discuss his issues with you." I told her, "I do not care what kind of disability he has. Clearly, he knows exactly what he is doing to my son. His disability isn't so bad that he doesn't understand the words "stop" and "no." I know he understands the sentence, "Leave me alone!"

The principal replied, "He doesn't have a mental disability, Charlena." I then asked, "What is the problem? Why isn't this little boy suspended or kicked out of the school?" They explained to me they couldn't talk about someone's child with another parent. I firmly told them, "I can come up with four options on why he isn't suspended. One, his family gives a lot of money to the school. Two, you do not know how to handle bullying, so you slide it under the rug. Three, you don't care, or Four, since my son is black, and the little boy is white, and this is a predominately white school, the little white boy is free to bully the black little boy. I am more than sure, that if the shoe was on the other foot, my son would have been suspended or kicked out of the school. So, which one is it?"

The principal started to cry and said I hurt her feelings. I looked directly at her without a smile and asked her, "So you are hurt? You are a grown woman and hurt by my words? If you are hurt by what I just said, how do you think my son feels when he is called names, when he is hit and bullied over and over again?" I told her, "Something has to be done and something needs to be done now!"

I didn't care that she was hurt. My son was hurting every single day.

She looked at me and didn't reply.

I then said, "Maybe, it is all of the above. It is sad that you have a teacher who works for your school who transferred her son because the same little boy, Vince, was bullying her son as well. With all due respect, that speaks a lot of volumes. The question is, why is Vince still here?"

The principal said, "Charlena, that is not the case. That is a different story."

I looked her in the eyes and said, "Sure it is. You kicked two little boys out of school because they defended themselves against, Vince. Although it was an extreme measure, as I recall, one little boy stabbed Vince with a pencil and other little boy choked Vince because Vince kept bullying them. Again, I ask you, why is Vince still enrolled in this school?"

Sadly, I did not receive a response that made a bit of sense.

Elijah fell into a dark state and started to shut me out. He didn't tell me too much of what was going on unless I forced it out of him by asking him over and over again. I would have to be creative by taking him to the park, bike riding, and skating – the normal things we always did, but I would have to change up the routine.

Elijah told me that when he was walking to art class, he bent down to tie up his shoes. A little girl said, "Look, everybody, look at Elijah tying his shoes. Let's kick him." He went on to say, "Mom, when everyone was walking into art class, they kicked me. They kicked me in the stomach, my ribs, and some of them kicked me in my head."

At that moment, my blood was boiling like lava in a volcano. "Elijah, what did you do?" I asked. He replied, "I tried covering my head. I tried rubbing and covering my stomach too, but when someone kicked me, I would cover whatever place they kicked me. I couldn't protect my whole body, I covered and rubbed what I could, because it hurt. After they were finished, I tied my shoes and walked into the classroom holding my head and stomach. I sat by myself. I told my art teacher, but she ignored me."

He went on to say, "I didn't cry. I held in my cry because I couldn't let them see me cry, but it hurt so bad."

I cried because I wasn't there to protect my baby. My baby was hurt and in pain, and I wasn't there to help him.

I took Elijah to the emergency room to get him checked out. They examined him and he had a dark bruise on his rib cage, but his rib wasn't broken. They noticed that when he urinated, he had blood in his urine. They ran tests, and the conclusion was that it was from him being kicked so many times in the same spot.

The next day, I had a talk with the art teacher, his other teachers, and the assistant principal. I wasn't surprised when they said they didn't have any clue about what happened. They did the most ridiculous thing ever. They called one of Elijah's classmate's parents to ask the child who Elijah was sitting with during art. I asked, "Are you serious? Are you really calling a child to ask her where Elijah was sitting?" I went on to say, "This is crazy and irrelevant." I then said, "So, Elijah made all of this up. You all are saying he kicked himself to the point he was urinating blood and had bruises on his rib cage. Also, the little girl that you called was the one who told everyone to kick Elijah." Again, the blame was placed on my child.

I left in a rage. I went to the police station and filed a report about what had happened. From that day forward, I went to the police station and filed a report on every incident. I was building a case for my son's protection.

I asked the principal if they could set up a parent-teacher conference with both parents because I felt as though maybe the child's parent wasn't aware of the situation. The principal acted as though that wasn't possible. She felt like things would escalate and get out of hand. I assured her that we are adults and we know how to control ourselves. She then said, "Charlena, we've talked to the other student's parents, and with that being said, we have taken care of the situation."

Her comment didn't sit well with me, because if the "situation" was taken care of, then why did the student continue to bully my son? The administrators in the school system need to put themselves in the parent's and student's shoes; I'm more than sure, if it was their children they would think differently.

I took matters into my own hands. If the principal wanted to keep the "situation" silent, to each its own, but as for me, I choose not to because my son was the one that was suffering on a daily basis. Not only was he suffering, but I too was suffering. I did not feel comfortable, at ease, or at peace, not knowing if I was going to see my son alive at the end of the day.

I looked in the parent's directory. However, I did not find Vince's parents' phone number, instead, I sent the child's mother an email, and asked her to call me at her earliest convenience. The child's mother called me back within five minutes of the email. I made her aware of what was going on, yet she acted as if she didn't have a clue.

After I spoke with her, I called the principal and told her I spoke with the parent and she said she wasn't aware of the situation. The principal then said, "Charlena, since you said she wasn't aware of the situation (the tone in her voice was basically saying I was lying about what the parent said). I corrected her and said, "That is not what I said, it came from the parent's mouth, that she wasn't aware of the situation at hand." The principal then said, "Charlena, I will get back with you by the end of the week."

As a concerned parent, I felt I had to break the silence because I knew the teachers and administrators weren't going to take my concerns to another level.

Silence isn't golden when it comes to our child's well-being and when they are being bullied; because a mind is a terrible thing to waste, especially at such a young age.

As parents, guardians, and educators we have to look out for the signs. Elijah's signs were: quietness, changes in mood, always jumpy, anxious, fear, shattered confidence, and a feeling of hopelessness. After I spoke with the little boy's mother things changed a bit, but not permanently.

My friend Vanessa's daughter, Sasha, was in the eleventh grade and she was a gifted student. However, Vanessa noticed Sasha's grades were dropping significantly. She also noticed her mood changed from hot to cold, bitter, quick-tempered, and always so unhappy. She fell into a state of depression and hardly ever talked. Vanessa noticed Sasha had begun stealing from her.

While Vanessa was getting ready for work, she yelled from upstairs, "Sasha, are you up and getting ready?" Sasha didn't answer. Vanessa went upstairs and found Sasha on the bathroom floor, foaming at the mouth. She called 911, then held her daughter in her arms until help arrived.

After they pumped the pills out of Sasha and she was stable, the social worker asked, "Sasha, what was your motive for taking an overdose?"

Sasha turned her back and didn't answer the question. Vanessa calmly asked her again. Sasha ignored her too. Vanessa cried and begged Sasha to please talk to her. However, Sasha didn't reply.

The social worker told Sasha she would give her a couple of days to recover. She told Sasha if she didn't receive an answer, she would feel she'd have no choice but to take Sasha out of her home and put her in a ward for children that harm themselves. She explained to Sasha, "We do not want you to hurt yourself again."

Seven days passed and Sasha was still silent. The nurses and physician came to treat her, but nothing was said. I visited Vanessa and Sasha every other day. Vanessa asked me to talk to Sasha; I hesitated because I didn't want to put pressure on her, and I didn't want her to go further into a deeper state of depression. I didn't want her to go deeper into the dark hole because of what was going on.

I asked Sasha was it okay for me to talk to her, she nodded her head yes with her back turned. I asked her would it be okay if I moved my chair towards her so I could see her. She nodded, yes. When I start talking to

Sasha, Vanessa and the social worker walked in the door. I asked Sasha was it okay if her mother and the social worker listened to our conversation. Once again, Sasha nodded her head, yes.

I started the conversation, "Sasha, I remember when you were young, you were filled with so much joy and happiness. You always looked at the clouds and made something exciting out of them. Do you remember that?" Sasha nodded her head yes and cracked a smile.

I said, "Yeah, I remember that too. I also remember how close you and your mother used to be. You always talked to her about anything and everything." I laughed and said, "You guys had a close-knit relationship, you were like two peas in a pod."

Sasha smiled and looked at her mother, then she started to tear up.

"What's wrong, Sasha?" I asked calmly with tears rolling down my cheek. I tried holding them in, but I instantly felt her pain.

Sasha, looked at Vanessa crying endlessly and said, "Mommy."

I got up and let Vanessa sit in my chair.

The social worker was in tears, she whispered and said, "Thank you so much for breaking the ice." I replied, "You're welcome, but the ice is far from being broken."

Vanessa put Sasha's hand in her hand, her voice was trembling, "Baby, I am here. I am always here. I never left. Talk to me."

When Sasha tried to talk, her throat was dry. She cleared her throat and softly asked for some water. After a sip, her voice cracked as she tried to talk. We could hardly understand what she was saying because she was crying so hard that it was tough to make out her words. "I am not sick. I love myself. I am just tired of the hurt and pain I go through every day at school. I thought if I take my life, I wouldn't have to go through the agony anymore. I am so sorry, Mommy. I hurt you. I am so sorry, Mommy if I made you cry. I am so sorry, Mommy for shutting you out. Mommy, I am so sorry. I am so sorry for being selfish. I just couldn't take it anymore."

"It's okay, Sasha. It's okay. Before it gets this far again, you have to come talk to me." Vanessa replied squeezing her hand tighter.

"School." Sasha stumbled on her words.

She tried it again, "School... School, Mommy is a nightmare. Those girls are so evil, and every day is a constant battle. It takes more out of me to get up in the morning than it does for me to study for all of my classes in one day.

I was jumped a couple of weeks ago in the bathroom by four girls because one of the girl's boyfriend likes me. Mommy, I do not like him. I am trying to get my work done so I can graduate high school. There is a rumor going around about me, people are calling me all kinds of names, and saying I've been with all the boys. Mommy, I am a virgin. The boys try to touch me because they think I am easy; I tell them to leave me alone. They ignore the word no.

I spoke to my teachers and counselor about it; they told me it wasn't rape, because they didn't force themselves on me. Mommy, they didn't, but I don't want them to touch me at all. When I answer questions in class my classmates throw gum, paper, pens, pencils, books or whatever they can. The teachers are scared of the students; they don't say anything, they keep on teaching as if nothing's happening.

Mommy, we are close, but I was too embarrassed to tell you what was going on. The pressure took over my mind because I couldn't go on like this every day. Even on social media, they posted my head on nasty disturbing images.

I am embarrassed to say this but one image was of me having oral sex and that wasn't me. The whole school knew of it, and they knew that wasn't me because the skin tone was darker. They copied and pasted the image. There's a rumor going around saying I have herpes and all kinds of STD's.

Mommy, that isn't true. Mommy, it's horrible. I am so sorry for stealing from you, I will pay you your money back. I used the money for the jukebox at a nearby restaurant. I skipped classes just to get away, but I did my work while I was at the restaurant. When you picked me up from school, some days I walked back to school to make it appear like I was walking out of the building.

I am so sorry, Mommy. I had to leave. If I didn't, I wouldn't be here today. I should have told you all of this, but I didn't have the heart. I thought if I took my life it would be easier."

Everybody in the room was crying, the physician walked into the room and heard most of the story but we didn't notice his presence.

Vanessa kissed Sasha's hands and said, "Baby, you know I would have taken care of this. I would have taken care of you. You know you can talk to me about everything. I am here for you always. I am so sorry you had to go through this alone. I am so sorry."

The physician verified that Sasha was a virgin and that she didn't have a Sexual Transmitted Disease.

"See, Mommy, I told you," Sasha said as her eyes filled with more tears.

"I believed you when you told me, Sasha," Vanessa replied.

The social worker called up an officer to file a report.

Silence isn't golden. When our children act out, we cannot assume what it may be. We have to have open communication with our children. We have to talk to them even if they feel as though we are being "nosy" or in their "business."

It's better to know than regret not asking. We have to find a way to ask and start searching for clues. We have to take time to talk to their teachers to see if they've noticed or seen anything unusual. If the teacher isn't much help, we have to talk to our children's friends to see if they've observed anything. Some of their friends we can't trust, but it doesn't hurt to ask, because the truth will come out eventually.

We have to notice the signs and the missing pieces. Normally, our children have a routine and form a pattern. Once the pattern or routine changes, we need to take note. If it's for the better, we need to ask questions and give them a compliment.

My oldest son's pattern changed for the better; I asked him what was going on because I saw a 'new and improved' Xavier. He said, "Mom, I am hanging with a new crowd of people and they are focused on their work, they participate in sports and clubs. I want to be successful. We help each other to reach our goals." I gave him a hug and told him I loved his way of thinking. He said, "Well, Mom, you always say, you are who you hang around with."

If your child's pattern has shifted for the worse, questions also need to be asked. Talk to your child to see what is going on, let he/she know that you care. More than likely, your child will have a "snappy attitude", but do not let the snappy attitude push you away. Their snappy attitude should give you more than enough reason to be anxious. You should extend an invitation to communicate, listen, understand, let them know you are here to listen, and that you are concerned.

Maybe they are acting out because they want to be heard and cannot find the words to tell you. They are crying for help from the inside. Keep in mind that actions speak louder than words – and silence isn't golden.

CHAPTER 4

What's Wrong with Me?

WHEN MY SON WAS in second grade, he asked me, "Momma, what is wrong with me? Why do people pick on me? Is it because of my skin color? Is it because I look weak? Is it because I am nice? Is it because I choose to walk away as opposed to fighting back? Maybe I need to change who I am as a person because who I am now isn't good enough."

It hurt me to my heart to hear my seven-year-old son ask his momma, "What's wrong with me?" I hugged him and told him he is perfect the way he is.

I looked him straight in the eyes and said, "Elijah, do you love the skin you're in?"

He replied, "Yes."

I asked him, "Do you think you are weak?"

He answered, "Yes, because my bully thinks I am weak because I do not talk or hit back."

I asked him again, "Elijah, do you think you are weak? I do not want to hear about what you think your bully thinks of you. Do you think you are weak?"

He paused for a minute and said "Well... If my bully wasn't around, I would think I am strong. No, I am not weak, I am strong, but when he is around, he thinks I'm weak."

I then asked Elijah, "Do you think you need to change who you are as a person?"

He said, "No, I love myself, but I think I need to change who I am because I think I am too nice. I need to be mean and a fighter."

I sat Elijah down and said, "You said you are not weak, you love the skin you're in, you love yourself and you love who you are as a person when your bully isn't around. When you think about it, you are perfect just the way you are. It seems as though your bully is the one who needs to change the person he has become. Maybe he was a sweet little boy and something or someone did something to him to make him act the way he does, but that isn't an excuse, because he needs help. When I talk to your teachers, they always say, "Elijah, is so humble, sweet, and respectful. When we talk, he always makes eye contact. We love Elijah."

I went on to say, "When we go to the store you always open the door for the older people or someone who's in need of help. You are always willing to ask if they need a helping hand."

He looked at me as if I was making up stories to make him feel better.

I looked at him and said, "Elijah, remember when a lady was in a wheelchair and you said, Momma, don't forget to open the door for her when she leaves."

Elijah smiled and said, "Yes, I remember that. I'm glad the store was small because if it was too big, I wouldn't have been able to keep my eyes on her. And when she checked out, I ran to the door and opened it for her."

I smiled at Elijah and said, "You sure did! And do you remember what she said?"

Elijah responded with a huge smile on his face, blushing at the same time, "She said wow, you are a beautiful young man who has a big heart." He went on to say, "She said I should share a small piece of my heart with the world because if they had a tiny piece of my heart the world would be a better place. Then she said thank you so much and never change who I am as a person because I am perfect just the way I am."

I smiled with tears in my eyes and said, "See, a stranger who didn't know anything about you said you shouldn't change because are perfect just the way you are!"

Elijah smiled and closed his eyes and said, "Yeah, I am perfect just the way I am."

I cannot stress this topic enough. As parents, we have to communicate with our children. Sometimes we have to go into great detail from the past and bring them to the present to remind them of how great of a person they are.

We have to be their "turbo-charge" to renew their positive thoughts. When our children are being bullied the words and wounds from the silent killer can make our children second-guess who they are as a person; they will begin to have thoughts of, what is wrong with "me?" Their subconscious mind will be filled with doubt, which will bring denial to the frontal lobe of their conscious mind. The frontal lobe is our brain control panel that focuses on our emotion, expression, dissects our personality, and is aware of the "judgment" that we see and hear from others.

The brain is a powerful force in the human body, therefore, what we see, hear, and feel are very critical. We have to be our children's guides when they are not strong enough to realize when someone is trying to put fear into their minds because the silent killer think they have the power to control our children's emotions or physical well-being.

The bad side effects of the words, "What is wrong with me?" plays a negative role in our children's lives, and it is not welcome. It causes our children to create self-doubt in their ability to accomplish anything. It shuts down their sense of imagination and creates darkness from fear that produces a dark cloud in our children's minds and over our children's heads.

The words, "What is wrong with me?" create a cardboard box in our children's minds and make them think there's no way out. Our children envision the box as self-acceptance by thinking the worst because of what someone said to them. We have to teach our children how to break out of the box, we have to let them know if they envision a box filled with self-doubt to open the box to let the sun come in.

The rays from the sun will restore their confidence, and the confidence will create and build a strong foundation of self-acceptance. Once the box is open, they will not need the flashlight that once was a temporary fix that they thought would protect them from their fears or the "boogie man." Once the box is open, they will shake off what grounded them in fear, they will have the courage to step out with confidence, smile, and be able to live the life that was once stolen from them.

We have to be our children's powerful force. We have to be the light that beams in slowly but surely, and sooner rather than later, we will be the bright sun to help rescue our children from the darkness of the silent killer.

As parents and guardians, we have to remember that timing is everything; if too much time passes, our children will find themselves in a dark, strange, unwelcome, and unexpected place.

We cannot have our children thinking, "What's wrong with me?" We have to save our children from slipping, we have to save our children from walking deeper and deeper into their thoughts of, "What's wrong with me?" We have to put a firm grip on our children. We have to hold on tight because we are our children's hope when they are in a dark place.

We are our children's roadmap when they think all is lost. We have to change their direction of drowning in self-doubt (What's wrong with me?). We have to destroy the hopeless feelings that are buried deep within our children. We, the parents, guardians, and educators have to be the wheels to put our children back on track. We are our children's guides and we have to put them back on the road of purpose.

One day, on vacation, I was watching my children at the poolside. I noticed a little boy, he had to be around six years old. He folded his towel very neatly. When he took off his sandals, I noticed he made sure they were aligned very neatly as well. When he took off his shirt, he folded it, he made sure the creases were perfect. There were some children in the pool who were chatting about him in a corner. A young girl, who looked as though she was in her early teenage years, yelled across the way, "Are you human or a robot?" The little boy ignored her question.

When the little boy jumped in the pool, he began to swim, he asked my daughter, niece, and son, if they want to throw his football together. They didn't mind. After a couple of minutes, he changed his mind and wanted only my daughter to play with him. My son and niece said, "Okay." They went on about their business and played in the lazy river.

Time passed and I told the kids to gather their belongings because I wanted to walk on the beach since the sun was setting. As we were walking out of the sliding door, I looked back and saw the group of kids starting to bully the little boy. Although the little boy thought they were playing as they splashed water on his face and took his football. I begin walking around, asking the adults that were sitting around the pool if they were the little boy's parents or guardian. Everyone replied, "No."

As I continued to ask, the older kids took it to another level and started to put his head underwater, asking him, "Are you a robot?" The little boy said, "No, I am not a robot. I just like my things to be perfect." The older kids said, "There's no such thing as perfect."

As I couldn't find the little boy's parents, I took control of the situation. I told the older kids in a firm voice, "Stop bullying him and give him his ball back. You wouldn't want anyone to treat you that way." The teenagers swam away.

The little boy looked relieved. I saw a couple of people sitting outside the pool area and asked them if they were the little boy's parents. They said, "Yes." I made them aware of what was going on, and they walked to the inside pool area to keep an eye on him.

Some people fail to realize that other people, despite their age, may have an Obsessive-Compulsive Spectrum Disorder, or maybe they just want things to be to their liking. That doesn't mean a person isn't human. Those older kids didn't think about that little boy's feelings. They didn't know what kind of damage (if any) they caused, because of the questions that they asked or how they treated the little boy by continuing to dip his head underwater.

The next day, the little boy was in the pool and he asked my daughter if she wanted to play with him. My daughter smiled. He said, "You do not have to pretend you want to play with me. You might think something is wrong with me because of what happened yesterday." Although my daughter was much older than the little boy, she played with him because she didn't want him to play alone.

Elijah said, "Momma, he reminds me of myself. We like to do things a certain way, different than other people. Now I see why he only wants to play with Sarah because Sarah always has a friendly and welcoming attitude. He wants to feel comfortable." I replied, "Yes, that is very true."

Elijah looked at me, then he looked at the little boy, he looked at me again and said "Mom, it is an awesome feeling to be different. Why would I want to be like anyone else but me?"

I smiled at Elijah and gave him a high five and said, "Hey, you better say it again!"

He laughed and repeated himself, this time he was louder than before.

I laughed and said, "You know, Elijah, it would be boring if everyone were so much alike. We need more people like us who dare to be different. We are the ones who make this world an extraordinary place!" He smiled and jumped in the pool.

We have to remind our children from time to time that it is okay to be different. I tell my children all the time we are different in our own unique way, and there is nothing wrong with that.

I tell them, sometimes the people who talked about you are the ones who want to be like you. They are jealous because they want what you have, or they admire something about you. They feel like if they can't be you, then they try to tear you down to shatter your confidence to make themselves feel and look good.

During an assembly at my children's school, one of the teachers asked the students what were their most challenging moments in middle school. I was surprised to hear some of the student remarks. A young girl started off by saying, "I have a couple of challenges I battle, but the one that stands out the most is feeling pressured to be someone I'm not."

Another student interrupted her and said, "I agree. I dress differently because a person's appearance is always judged. I wear make-up. I always get the latest phone. And I make sure I have the hottest shoes because I have to keep up with the latest trend."

There were other students talking among each other. The students were getting louder and louder; a teacher raised his hand and said, "Okay, calm down. Only one person can talk at a time."

A young man said, "When my classmate's joke around, sometimes that's challenging because I know they really mean what they saying about me."

A student said, "Well, Robert, you do have big teeth and a lazy eye."

The students laughed. A teacher took the student who made the outburst out of the auditorium. The principal asked the students to calm down. She went on to say, "Hey, you guys, this is a serious matter and it should be taken seriously. We are trying to have an understanding of your challenges in school so we can help. We're trying to understand where to start so we can help resolve your challenges."

Another young girl started the conversation, stood up and said, "The challenges started when I was in elementary school. I loved who I was but I was bullied by my peers. When I told my teachers, they ignored me. When I talked to my parents about it, they talked to my teachers, but apparently, they ignored them too. I thought I solved the problem by changing who I was as a person. I felt like something was wrong with me, so I changed my clothes, I got my nails done, cut my hair, and changed everything about me to fit in. Until this day, the old me is somewhere in here who wants to come out, but I won't let her because I settled for the person who I am today. And most importantly, I solved the problem, because my peers don't bully me anymore."

A young man stood up and said, "My challenges started in elementary school too." He looked down and said, "Well they weren't challenges, let me call it for what it was. I was being bullied and it went unheard. So today, I am a person that my (he used his fingers to quote friends) "friends" made me. They so do not know the real Justin, but I do. I must say, sometimes I lose myself for being someone I'm not."

Before I knew it, there were a lot of students standing up telling their story, and the cause of their challenges was the silent killer — the bully.

A young man spoke up and said, "When I was in fourth grade I was knocked down and suffered a concussion. I woke up in the nurse's office. I remembered what happened. I was playing on the playground and one of my classmates tried to untie my fingers on the monkey bars. He wasn't supposed to be climbing on top of the monkey bars in the first place.

I jumped down and told my teacher. She said, "Marcus maybe he's trying to play with you, go play with someone else or play by yourself." I tried to tell her what really happened but she talked over me and started to yell at me for no reason, she said, "Marcus, I said go and play!" I remember hanging upside down on the jungle gym while my classmate purposely stepped on my fingers when I tried to climb up.

Next thing I knew, I landed head first and blacked out. That's when I woke up in the nurse's office. If teachers pay attention to the students and listen to us instead of brushing us off, we wouldn't be damaged because of what someone has done to us in the past."

Everyone was silent until a young lady by the name of Aja spoke out and said, "I always felt like something was wrong with me because I was always called stupid or four-eyed because I wore glasses. To add insult to injury, I was jumped in elementary school by three girls who took my glasses and stepped on them. They put bubble gum in my hair and twisted my braids together in knots and the last thing I remember they kicked me senseless because I began to see double before I faded in the background.

After that, I didn't remember anything. I woke up in the hospital with a broken arm. I agree, Justin, the teachers never listen to the students. I used to tell my teachers what was going on, but they ignored me too.

After someone's hurt, that is when they do something about it, but what if when the person gets hurts and it is worse than a broken arm? What if that person dies? It could have been prevented if the teachers would have listened."

Aja was quiet for a minute. Then she said, "And my parents went up to the school plenty of times and nothing was done. They tried transferring me to another school, but I couldn't attend because it was either full or it wasn't in my district. They tried home-schooling, but it was too late to register and I was put on the waiting list. My parents did all they could do, but just like you said, Justin, they were ignored too."

The stories that were told by the students were heartbreaking.

One student confronted the teachers in a respectful way. He said, "With all due respect, bullying happens here and nothing is done. The teachers ignore us here too. You guys always say talk it out, but sometimes we need a teacher to take action and discipline the student who is being the bully. What I hate most is when the innocent students start to take up for ourselves, we are the ones who get in trouble. We are the ones who have to go to the main office to get a referral.

When will the students be heard, not only heard but taken seriously? Our issues matter too. We are told we do not have problems because we are too young. We have problems too and most of the time it comes from either another student, it could be from home, and sometimes it's from the teachers."

The student went on to say, "I've been bullied by a teacher before and nothing was done."

One of the male teachers cut the young man off and said, "Hold up, hold up, Brandt. Let's not get too carried away and place blame."

Brandt then said, "See, this is a prime example. The student voices are never heard. If you don't like what you hear you shut us down or cut us off. How is that fair?"

Two teachers started to walk towards Brandt, but Brandt sat down and humbled himself before the teachers approached him.

A young girl in a yellow shirt asked, "Why don't the teachers hear the students out? Why is it that the teachers are always right and the students are wrong? Is that fair to us, the students?"

She went on to say, "Sometimes as a student, it makes me feel like something is wrong with me. It makes me second-guess myself to think that I was wrong, but after I think about it, I realized that I wasn't wrong.

However, when I speak up, I am told I'm being disrespectful. How is that? When I am only trying to explain so everyone will have an understanding. What makes matters worse, when the teachers talk to our parents, most of the time, they change up the story. Sometimes the teachers are wrong and the students are right. I am glad I have parents who don't believe everything the teachers say. Can a teacher here answer my question?"

I was waiting for a teacher to respond. The principal took over and said, "Well, sometimes we want to know exactly what happened. We want to talk to you and the teacher. With that being said, we listen. We just want to know what happened so we have both parties' interests at heart. We want to be fair."

All of the students were talking at the same time, and most of them were upset. One student said, "Fair. The students are blamed for everything that goes wrong. The teachers make it seem like it's something wrong with us. We just want to be heard."

Again, the teachers silenced the students. The assistant principal announced that she was going to cut the assembly short and the students were going to head back to class by grade.

What I noticed was, when the students started to speak up and tell the truth the educators did not want to hear them. How is that fair to the students?

As the students were walking out of the auditorium, I heard them talking amongst each other, saying here and there, "See, I do not understand why they ask us what our challenges are, they don't care. They only care if it's not about them."

A young girl replied, "Yeah if we were saying something positive about them, they wouldn't cut the assembly short. I do not understand why they never want to hear their faults. How can they make it right if they don't want to know? You're right, they do not care. Not at all."

I overheard a group of students saying, "See, they always make it seem like something is wrong with us when they are the ones who never want to hear the truth."

The students were going on and on saying, "Why bother to ask if they are not going to at least listen and try to solve the problem? It's always their way or no way at all. They always want to talk about what we are doing wrong."

When I walked out the door, I heard a young girl tell her friend, "Well, this was a waste of time. I can't wait to leave this school. I am going to ask my mom to home-school me next year."

After listening to the children in the assembly, I heard them suffocating from deep within. Why should our children feel like something is wrong with them, whether the cause is their classmates or their educators?

When our children leave home to go to school, they are fighting an uphill battle, and we have to reinforce over and over again and let our children know we are here to listen to whatever they are going through.

As parents and guardians, we have to dissect what our children go through very carefully, and we have to look at each angle because as we all know, lies can't live forever. We have to remind our children that they are important to us. We have to teach them how to stand their ground and reassure them that they will not have to stand alone.

Our children are a reflection of us, we have to lead by example and let them know there isn't anything wrong with them. We have to instill in them that it is important and it is okay for them to step into their truth because they are unique, and they do not have to walk in someone else's shoes.

As parents and guardians, we have to be bold and tell them if they attempt to walk in anyone else shoes, they are going to be highly disappointed because the shoes they are trying to walk in won't fit.

Our children are extraordinary. They are filled with grace, integrity, and determination, and because they are a reflection of their parents, they shouldn't have to think something is wrong with them, nor should they have to sacrifice their personality, character, and well-being to make someone else feel worthwhile.

We need to firmly tell our children in a loving way that they do not have to tear themselves down to make someone else feel good because they are fabulous just the way they are.

Our Children's Voices Matter

I HAVE NOTICED THAT an adult's voice is paid more attention to than a child's voice. Some people fail to realize, just because an adult is older, that doesn't mean they are always right. In my household, my children have a voice. They are entitled to voice their opinion in a respectful way. A child's voice deserves to be heard too, regardless of age.

My children and I have open communication. I feel it is important to listen to your children's opinions and concerns. After my children voice their opinion, we either agree, apologize, or we come to a decision to agree to disagree and/or compromise (depending on the situation).

Over the course of the years, I've learned that parents are not always right. We have our faults as well. Therefore, listening to your children and apologizing if needed isn't the end of the world. Apologizing is saying, I want the best for you, I am human, and I am not perfect. It also helps our children understand that parents make mistakes too.

Listening to our children applies to the teachers as well. From my experiences at my children's school, some of the teachers and administrators are very passive towards the students when there's a conflict. I am a firm believer that teaching and learning begin at home. However, I also stand firm that every child's voice deserves to be heard too.

My daughter was very disturbed when I picked her up from school. I had never seen her so upset and hurt. She was crying so badly that it was hard for me to understand what she was saying. I had to tell her to breathe slowly. Once she got herself together, she gathered her thoughts and told me what had happened. "Mom, today I felt violated and powerless." I quickly cut her off and asked her if she had been sexually harassed. She said, "No." I asked because the words "violated" and "powerless" are very powerful words.

Sarah went on to say, "I took my chips with me to recess. I forgot I had them in my hand because I was talking to my friends. When I stepped one foot outside, I was told by one of the teachers not to take my chips outside. I listened and took my chips back to the classroom. I hesitated because I knew a teacher wasn't in the room, but I thought I would run in and run right back out."

Ms. Rogers quickly snapped and said, "Sarah, what are you doing in the classroom alone?" I tried to explain but I wasn't able to get my words out, because Ms. Rogers cut me off.

She yelled at me, saying, "Sarah, you know a student is not allowed to be in the classroom alone." I looked at her and tried to explain it again. When I opened my mouth to speak, she cut me off again and said, "Sarah, I do not want to hear what you have to say because there isn't an excuse." I tried to explain again, that time I got the word "but" out, and again, Mom, she cut me off, saying, "There is no 'but'—I don't want to hear that word because you know you are not allowed in the classroom alone."

Sarah went on to say, "Mom, I felt powerless because she didn't let me explain. Either way, I was going to be blamed because I mistakenly took my chips outside. I was told to put my chips away, so I took them to the classroom to put them away. I admit I was at fault for going in the classroom alone, but I put my chips in my backpack and walked right out until Ms. Rogers rudely scolded me.

I felt violated because I am not used to not having a voice. I really was crushed because she didn't give me an opportunity to explain myself. She wouldn't let me get one word out. That wasn't fair. I felt like I was backed in a corner without anywhere to turn. And what made matters worse, I had to apologize to her for being in the classroom without an adult there."

I had never seen my daughter so disturbed. I emailed Ms. Rogers and the principal about the issue. Ms. Rogers and I went back and forth sending unpleasant emails for a couple of days. I was surprised the principal didn't interfere with the emails that were sent. I'd had enough of the senseless emails. Ms. Rogers emailed me about anything and everything; except about what happened a couple of days ago. I wanted to meet face to face. I set up a parent-student-teacher conference because the things that were said by email didn't sit well with me.

The assistant principal was the mediator during the conference. Ms. Rogers started the conference off by talking about Sarah's grades. I politely said, "With all due respect, we are not here to talk about her grades. As a matter of fact, we spoke with her advisor last week about her grades, which are pretty good, I might add. We are here to talk about the bag of chips situation.

I'm sure you are aware of the tone of voice that was used. I am also sure, you remember you didn't give Sarah an opportunity to explain herself. Before you start to point the finger, Sarah, told me that she wasn't allowed in the classroom without a teacher present. I told Sarah, if she knew she wasn't allowed in the classroom she should have thrown her chips in the trashcan and abided by the rules, which clearly she didn't."

I went on to say, "Ms. Rogers, what I am trying to understand is why did you scold my daughter? Why didn't you listen to what Sarah had to say? Maybe it wouldn't have gotten this far if you'd taken time to listen."

Ms. Rogers replied, "Ms. Jackson, I didn't yell at Sarah. I was upset with her because she knew she wasn't supposed to be in the classroom without supervision."

I looked at Ms. Rogers, saying to myself, *do not play with me, because today is not the day.* I then replied, "Ms. Rogers, thank you for your answer, but let's nipped it in the bud. You did scold my daughter. Sarah was very upset the other day. Since you are not going own up to what you did, I am letting you know I know you yelled at my daughter in a rude and disrespectful way. Whatever your answer is, that didn't give you a reason to scold my child. Not to mention, you didn't give her an opportunity to explain. She could have been trying to tell you something important like there was a fire, or someone was sick, who knows? I guess we will never know because you didn't give her the opportunity to explain herself."

Ms. Rogers replied, "Well, Ms. Jackson, she shouldn't have been in the classroom alone, because she could have put herself in danger, or worse."

I answered, "That is very true. However, if a person isn't given the opportunity to explain, we cannot assume either."

I went on to say, "Ms. Rogers, in my household my children have a voice. They are entitled to speak their opinion because as an adult and parent I am not always right. I talked to Sarah about her error but I am going to talk to you about your error as well. You, as the adult, should have let her explain why she was in the room. This is not the first time Sarah has come to me to tell me about you not giving the students the opportunity to speak, or you scolding the students. That is when stasis starts to take place, because the teachers/adult thinks since they are older, they can talk to the students any kind of way, and that's the end of the conversation."

I then said, "Ms. Rogers, this is where the problem lies, the teachers and adults do not respect the students. Now, if you feel like you can disrespect the students, do you think they are going to respect you?"

She looked at me and said, "Maybe. Maybe not."

I replied, "Ms. Rogers, more than likely they are not going to respect you. And if they respect you, they too will have a breaking point."

She looked at me as if she didn't care, or she simply didn't understand. I gave her the benefit of the doubt and took it as she didn't understand. With that being said, I explained the word 'respect' with a situation I'd found myself in at my oldest son's school.

"Ms. Rogers, as you might not know, my oldest son is in high school, and as I was talking to the nurse, she rudely cut off our conversation, walked up to a student, got in his face and yelled, "Chad, pull up your damn pants. I am so sick and tired of telling you to pull your pants up every damn day."

The student then yelled at her and cursed her out too. They constantly went back and forth. I hesitated, but I had to interrupt them both because it was ridiculous how they were talking to each other. I looked the young man in the eye and said calmly, "Why do you come to school every day with your pants down, knowing this is what you are going to hear every single day? Aren't you tired of hearing this?"

The young man was mad, he was moving from side to side. I looked at him and said, "Calm down, it's okay."

The nurse said, "Ms. Jackson, just so you know, you are wasting your time talking to him."

The young man started to huff, he was about to say something until I said, "Don't look at her and do not say anything. She wants you to say something back. Look at me and answer my question."

He was still moving from side to side. He looked at me, then he looked down and said, "I do not have a belt."

I looked at him and said, "Well, use your shoelaces. Why would you want to come to school to listen to this every single day?"

The young man said, "Then I won't have shoelaces in my shoes."

I said to him, "You will get through the day. Make up your mind. Do you want them to pull you to the side all day, yelling, and getting you all upset for not having on a belt?"

He shrugged, basically saying he didn't care.

I looked at him and said, "Okay, the choice is yours."

The nurse looked at him, but she was talking to me and said, "See, I told you, you were just wasting your time."

After I talked to the nurse the young man said, "Excuse me, Ms. Lady." He lifted up his shirt and said, "I chose to take the shoelaces out my shoes and use them as a belt."

I smiled, gave the young man a hug, and said, "That was an awesome choice."

I looked at the nurse and said, "See, if you take the time to talk to the students, you will learn something about them. Some will listen, and some might not. However, if you give them a chance, you never know what you might get."

I walked away, but then I turned around and said, "Last but not least, Chad didn't raise his voice to me because I didn't raise my voice to him. I respected him because I wanted to be treated the same way in return. You see, it's all about how you talk to people. If you treat them with respect, more than likely you will be given the same respect you put out."

She looked at me with her lip curled and said, "These are children, they're supposed to respect adults."

I replied, "You don't understand, and that's fine. We all learn at our own pace."

Later that day, I went to the Goodwill and purchased a belt for Chad. I gave it to my son to give him the next day.

Weeks later I saw Chad, he said, "Ms. Lady, what's your name?"

I said, "Hello Chad! My name is Ms. Jackson."

He said, "You remember my name."

I replied, "How can I forget an extraordinary person, who's going to make a difference in the world?"

He smiled and said, "Ms. Jackson, thank you for the belt. I wear it every day. My mother does the best she can do, and I try not to bother her about my needs because she has a lot on her plate."

I gave him a hug and said, "Chad, you are more than welcome."

I went on to say, "Make sure you focus on your schoolwork. Make your mother proud."

Ms. Rogers looked at me like she didn't care. I could tell the assistant principal took note because it showed in his facial expression.

I ended the conference by saying, "Instead of blaming the students we first need to take time to listen. As adults, we need to stop abusing our power. We also need to eliminate the mindset that we're always right. We have to take the time to listen. If we take time to listen, believe it or not, it will make a huge difference."

Weeks went by and Sarah told me she saw an improvement with Ms. Rogers' words and actions towards her and her fellow classmates. Which in my opinion was amazing. Everybody can make room for growth and everyone has the opportunity to change.

I know some teachers feel as though maybe an elementary, middle, or high schooler doesn't have any problems. They might think their issues are petty and simple. However, that isn't true; I learned from my children the issues they have, whether big or small, bother them deeply.

Just like an adult, children need to vent, they need and want to express themselves but sometimes they are treated unfairly because they are not given the opportunity to express themselves because of their age.

My oldest and youngest sons were bullied when they were in kindergarten but their little voices would go unheard because their complaints weren't being taken seriously in their teacher's or administrator's eyes. When I had a parent-teacher conference, some of the teachers would act as if they didn't know anything about what happened, or some would act like they were concerned, just because I (the parent) was there seeking a solution to the problem. Which I failed to believe; if they had listened, they would have known exactly what had happened and the problem would have been solved without the parent stepping in.

From my experience, I do not understand why some teachers and/or parent/guardians tell their children to tell someone when most of the time telling the teacher falls on deaf ears. Sometimes parent/guardians are too busy to listen as well because they had a rough day and do not feel like being bothered.

We as parents need to do our part. Some parents know exactly what is going on but they neglect to listen to their children. Some parents prefer to only listen to the teachers, nip it in the bud, and feel like the problem is solved. However, the parent/guardian neglects to ask their child what happened. They neglect to ask their child how he or she feels. The child is pushed to the side and/or ignored.

Sometimes a parent/guardian wonders why their child is behaving badly or why they are hard to control. It's because the child isn't being heard, they feel like their voices don't matter; and at that point in time, the child says to himself or herself, "What's the use?"

Children's feelings shouldn't be ignored. They shouldn't have the mindset of "It is what is it." When children feel like they do not matter, they act out, their confidence is shattered, and they feel like they do not have anything to live for or nothing to lose.

I am not perfect, but one thing's for sure; when my children need to talk, they know they can talk to me about what is going on in their lives. There are days when I am beyond tired, and I'll ask them, "Can it wait?" or

"Is it important?" Most of the time, they will say, "Mom, it is important." When they tell me it's important, I stop whatever I am doing and I sit down and listen.

When they tell me it can wait, most of the time they forget, and I have to ask them what they wanted to talk about. We have to be involved in our children's lives. We have to let them know they count and their voices matter.

There are some parents who listen to their children and only their children. Those are the parents who make excuses for their children's outrageous behavior. Those children are the ones who are in control of the household. They are the ones who are unmanageable because they are verbally abusive to their parents, and they are the ones who make the decisions in their household.

Most of the time, those are the children who are disrespectful to the teachers because they are disrespectful to their parents.

There was a little girl in my daughter's class who always acted out. I never understood why until one day, she opened her lunch box and noticed she had the wrong snack in her bag. She asked the teacher if she could call her mother. When her mother came to the classroom to bring the right snack, the little girl verbally abused her mother, she told her mother she hated her for putting the wrong snack in her bag. She made a scene in the hallway and interrupted the entire fourth and fifth-grade floor. The little girl's mother brought the snack the little girl wanted to eat. The little girl told her mother, "I still hate you, and you better not make this mistake again."

I was shocked to hear the little girl talk to her mother with such vile language. I knew then that the child ran the household and there weren't any rules and regulations or consequences the child would endure later.

As parents and guardians, we have to know that there is a fine line between letting our children speak their mind in a respectful way and when our children are being disrespectful. There should be rules and regulations our children should abide by, and yes, our children's voices deserve to be heard, but there is a way of going about things the right way.

Overall, there are boundaries that have to be set. No, a child shouldn't feel like their feelings are not important. A child shouldn't be having sleepless nights. A child shouldn't be stressed or depressed; they should be living a bubbly, joyful, and happy life. They should have an imagination that is out of this world and is filled with limitless possibilities.

With that in mind, every situation needs to be dissected. Nothing should be taken lightly, our children's voices deserve to be heard; parents, guardians, and teachers should make their expectations clear and have an understanding of what was said and done. And everyone should be given the opportunity to have a fair trial and to be treated with dignity and respect.

· CHAPTER 6 ·

Enough is Enough

WHY DO OUR CHILDREN have to struggle to fly because the bullies think they have the ability to clip their wings? What will it take for some parents, guardians, teachers, and higher authorities to pay attention to the red flags and acknowledge what is really going on? How much does a person have to endure before they break down mentally and spaz out, or before someone suffers a tragic loss?

Bullying is overlooked in the worst way. However, the evidence is relevant; it is standing right in front of you and staring you in the face. It is standing right behind you as it breathes on your neck. It gives our children chill bumps because it knows it has the power to destroy.

Its powers are getting stronger because it is killing our children. It tears our children down, and it makes our children feel like they are the victims. It enables them to see the truth because it is too busy harassing our children with their threats by putting suicidal thoughts in our children's minds.

When will we wake up and see that the silent killer is killing our children? When will we open our eyes to see that we are the reason why the silent killer is powerful? We, the children's parents, guardians, teachers, school administrators, and higher authorities are the ones who are giving the silent killer its powers because we ignore what we see; we ignore what we hear, we procrastinate by forgiving the silent killer, and by giving it too many chances, one after another. When will we realize that the silent killer isn't only manipulating our children but it is controlling us too?

After going back and forth with my son's teachers and higher authority about the same issues that continued to occur with the same little boy, I thought to myself, maybe there is but so much the teachers and higher authority can do. However, I strongly believe they could have suspended the little boy. I was told by the higher authority, just because I do not see a change, that doesn't mean that nothing is being done. However, I was beyond furious because clearly, nothing was being done.

I reached out to the little boy's mother again. I thought maybe she didn't understand our first conversation. I explained to her once again what was going on. I also emailed her for proof that I'd contacted her and/or just in case she digests reading about the bullying problem better than listening or hearing a verbal message.

During our conversation, she made it known that her son wasn't racist, and that her son wanted to have a playdate with Elijah. She went on to say, "I sent you an invite, but you never responded." I sat in my car and collected my thoughts. Clearly, she wasn't understanding the serious matter that was at stake here.

I told her I wasn't going to let my son play with someone who tortured him on a daily basis; which was the importance of the call. I calmly explained to her what her son was saying and doing to my son. Her son is three times bigger than my son; as a matter of fact, he is bigger than every student in the entire grade. I explained to her, I think he knows that and takes advantage by bulling Elijah and his other classmates.

She was in denial, and I knew right then and there the conversation was falling on deaf ears. I calmly talked to her about the issue, "Your son calls my son names, he put his hands on him, he once tripped him and he fell down the stairs." I made it clear to her that her son does all of these things purposely. I went on to say, "Your son does these things to other students as well."

She didn't want to acknowledge what was going on; out of the blue, she said, "Well, my son says your son bullies him." I asked her, "Is that so? If it is, why didn't you tell me that when I called and emailed you the first time?" I respectfully told her, "I am coming to you as a concerned parent and I want you to talk to your son because I want my son to have a good day at school."

Again, she was in denial. Towards the end of the conversation, I reminded her that the principal spoke with her and her husband about every incident that had occurred (when she and I spoke the first time, she acted as if she was clueless about what was going on). She paused. I said, "I know you are aware because the principal made it clear that one of the teachers walked your son to your car during car riders because she saw your son trip my son on the steps." She said, "Well, I wasn't aware of that situation." I reminded her, "Well, that was a couple of weeks ago, and I am sure you are aware of all of the situations that occurred."

I made it clear to her, "Whether you want to believe it or not is up to you. However, one thing's for sure, since first grade your son has been a bully to my child and other children for three years." I went on to say, "They weren't in the same grade in second grade and your son still managed to get to my son, whether it was during lunch, recess, or the carpool line."

I went on to ask, "When will enough be enough?"

She said, "Well, my son has been bullied too. He was choked and stabbed with a pencil."

I told her, "I remember that incident. The reason why he was choked and stabbed with a pencil was because he bullied both of the little boys over and over again to the point that your son pushed them to their breaking point. They were kicked out of school. However, your son caused them to defend themselves, yet your son is still causing problems and bullying other students. What makes matters worse is that one of the teachers who works at the school transferred her son to another school because your son was bullying her son as well. Also, there were other little boys who your son bullied who transferred to another school. And let me remind you again, the little boy who stabbed your son with a pencil was kicked out because he was defending himself against your son."

I said in a firm voice, "Look at the common denominator. Your son holds all the cards, yet parents transfer their children to keep them safe from your son. One child was kicked out of school because he was tortured by your son. My son is being bullied by your son as well. Yet your son still attends school and bullies my child and other students. I know as a parent you do not want to see or know the truth, but the truth is staring you directly in the face. Own it and take care of it."

She still was in denial.

I told her, "Let me make this clear, you son isn't running my son out of school, and just to let you know, I have collected police reports on your son, and my son is in Tae Kwon Do, and if your son touches him again my son will defend himself. I will not be responsible for any medical bills, because I have documents in writing that your son has bullied my son for three years. Since the school and higher authorities do not want to acknowledge the serious problem at hand, I told my son to defend himself. I suggest you talk to your son if you do not want him to get seriously hurt."

She went on to say, "Are you serious? You filed police reports on a kid?" I said firmly, "I sure did, and if my son says your son bullied him today, I will file another one. Please, make time to speak with your son."

The silent killer smells fear from our children, parents, guardians, teachers, school administrators, and higher authorities. It knows its actions are taken lightly because so many people are passive about how it paralyzes our children's mental state. Yet, so many people see the damage it causes and turn a blind eye to the scars and burdens our children carry as they sink deeper into a dark place.

There were plenty of times I had a serious talk with Elijah. After I had "that talk" with him, things changed. Elijah didn't want to fight back physically, and sometimes he didn't want to fight back verbally. I had to tell him it was time for him to stand up, fight back, and make sure his bully felt exactly what he was feeling.

I told Elijah, "When you are being bullied it seems very loud and speaks volumes because it takes control over your thoughts, and you give it power if you continue to let it go on. Silence has a louder roar than the bully, and that is when you have to say enough is enough."

Elijah looked as though he didn't understand.

I took Elijah to the bathroom and said, "Elijah, look in the mirror. Do you like what you see?"

He looked down. I said, "No, Elijah, look yourself directly in the eye. Do you like what you see?"

He looked at himself and said, "I like what I see."

His voice faded when he said, "But I do not like the way I feel. Inside I am not alive. Inside I am in the dark and sometimes it is hard for me to think. I am not happy. It shows on the outside as well. I feel like Vin's words have taken over me and the person who I really am is in a cage and can't get out."

He looked himself in the mirror and asked, "How do I get out?"

He turned around and looked at me and said, "Momma, how do I get out of the cage? When will I get out of the cage?"

I looked at Elijah and said, "Bullying makes a loud noise, but when you look at that person, they aren't saying anything. They are scared straight and they think that bullying someone else makes them look and feel good. Most of the time, their purpose is to bully other people so nobody will bully them. Bullies are cowards and hiding in disguise because they are lying to themselves and other people."

I went on to say, "Elijah, silence is good at times, but in this situation, it is dangerous, because the silence can be so loud to the point where you can't think straight. And if you do think, you are thinking for too long, and you start to think wrong."

He looked and said, "Vince is scared. When someone hits him back, he always cries and tells the teacher. He knows how to play the game. He acts like the victim. I want to hit him back, but he is a huge boy."

I looked at Elijah and said, "That is his only advantage and he feeds on it. He might be bigger than you, but you are quicker."

Elijah laughed.

I said, "You asked me, how do you get out of the cage. I can only give you my advice, and my advice is, when you've had enough you will break the silence. Silence is more than being quiet, believe it or not, it has a different type of roar. Silence observes, listens, and defends itself when people least expect it. I call it the "silent roar of confidence.""

Elijah smiled and repeated, "Silent roar of confidence."

I said, "Yes sir, silence has a louder roar that overcomes fears. It lets you know when you have had enough."

I explained to Elijah, "All of the hurt that is bottled inside is not healthy, and silence is a strange place to be when it is an unknown place where you can't recognize who you are." I became emotional as I told Elijah that he had to rise from the fire and heal himself from the hurt, pain, and self-doubt. I went on to say, "All that was said to you and about you by the bully are all lies, and one thing's for sure, lies do not live on forever."

Elijah said, "My teacher made him apologize a couple of times but I noticed he is forced to say he's sorry. If a person is made to say it, that means they are not saying I'm sorry because they mean it, they are saying it because they are forced to apologize."

I pondered on what to say, but I knew that I couldn't sugar-coat my advice. I agreed with Elijah and said, "Honestly, Elijah, sometimes when people apologize it isn't good enough. After they apologize their actions should improve. In his case, his actions are getting worse."

I looked Elijah in the eyes and said, "You are right. When a person is made to do something over and over again and has never changed, more than likely they are not sincere."

Elijah, said "I feel like I am being punished for something I didn't do. I didn't ask for this. I never was his friend. He started picking on me for no reason."

Elijah and I walked outside and sat on the porch.

Elijah, paused for a moment and looked at up the sky and said, "Momma, look at the cloud. Doesn't it look like a teardrop?"

I replied, "It sure does!"

Elijah's expression and body language shifted gears. He said, "Momma, my bully makes me feel like crap. He wants to see me break, but the only thing that is going to break around here is my silence. I am tired of feeling like a prisoner. I never stole anything from him but he has stolen a lot from me. All he has done is take from me. He's taken my happiness, taken my confidence, taken my freedom; and I am not taking it anymore."

He was on a roll when he said, "None of this is my fault. He wants to make it seem like everything is my fault. Momma, I didn't ask for this. I mind my business every day and he crowds my space. I am taking back the peace that he stole from me. If I have to fight for my peace, I will, because it is mine to have and it is not for him to hold or borrow. It belongs to me."

He paused for a minute and said, "Momma, as I look at the teardrop it has given me the strength to say enough is enough. It has given me the strength to get out of the cage. He will not see me fall apart, because I am taking it all back. I have had enough and it stops right here, and it is going to start with me standing up and taking charge."

I must say after talking to the bully's mother things were better; until one day, her son got a taste of his own medicine.

One of Elijah's teachers called me and said, "Ms. Jackson, I know I shouldn't be telling you this but I want you to tell Elijah that I am very proud of him for taking up for himself today. I saw what happened, and I know that this has been a journey for Elijah and I am so happy Elijah finally had enough."

She was so excited and emotional at the same time she stumbled over her words as she said, "The student somehow got Elijah's bookbag and hit Elijah with it. Elijah tripped or missed a step because he was trying to keep his balance. The student called Elijah all kinds of names. Elijah asked this little boy to stop a couple of times, so did I and other teachers as well. Next thing I knew, Elijah caught the student's foot and pulled a move on him and tied the student up somehow with his clothes. I wanted to call you to let you know what happened, and we made the other parent aware too."

Elijah told me what happened. He was happy he'd defended himself, but he said, "Momma, it's really sad that I had to go there."

I replied, "It is, Elijah, it really is, but sometimes we have to go there to let people know that enough is enough." I told him, "Believe me when I say you shook him up because he didn't see what you did coming, and he will leave you alone from now on. Sometimes people need a triple dose of their own medicine, and they will realize that it is not a good feeling to be humiliated, to be hurt emotionally and physically. I am proud you, Elijah, and do not be ashamed of what you did, because you had to take up for yourself. If not, he was going to continue to bully you. You have two years left in elementary and I bet the next two years are going to be peaceful."

After Elijah defended himself, we didn't have any problems with his bully again. However, the higher authority wanted to address the fight. I was more than happy to have a meeting with everyone. I laid everything out on the table and told them, "Every last one of you should be ashamed of yourselves. A third-grader had to fight for his peace because his voice wasn't being heard." I told them that little boy deserved everything he got, he bullied my son for three long years. I fought for my son for those three years and yet none of them listened.

"What did you want? My son to be buried either from being beaten and possibly killed, or commit suicide so you guys can cover up and bury the real issue, which is bullying. My son had had enough! It was better the little boy was tied up as opposed to my son hurting him to the point where both students would have been at the point of no return. My son or this little boy could have been permanently damaged for life.

Not to mention, who knows whether my son has been permanently damaged from three years of being bullied? Instead of confronting me about my son finally defending himself, you need to look at the problem. The problem is that you, as the higher authorities, are failing the students, and the parents who are in denial are failing their children. Parents, such as myself, and the students have to jump over hurdles and go through so many obstacles just to have a meeting, only to hear one excuse after another."

I continued, "I am happy my son is alive, breathing, and well. I am happy my son didn't harm the little boy badly. However, one thing's for sure, you all need to open your eyes and fix the problem. Stop taking bullying lightly, because next time you will have a bigger problem on your hands from someone else."

I didn't want to hear what they had to say, because I'd heard enough of "nothing" for years. I walked out of the room proudly. My voice probably wasn't heard but one thing for sure I knew they knew my son and I had had enough. We were together on the same page and we weren't going to tolerate this crap anymore.

There are so many parents who have had enough, and wonder when will there be an end to bullying. I know many parents asked when would change come and when would enough be enough. We have to keep roaring louder and louder by any means.

We have to gather unimaginable strength to battle these cowards, even though we can clearly see that some parents, guardians, teachers, school administrators, and higher authorities are living a carefree life; they come up with unreasonable excuses and lies that only make sense to themselves.

As the ones who care, we have to speak louder to save our children and keep their innocence. We have to make changes by empowering others and giving those who are afraid to speak up a reason to release their fears. We have to help them see that enough is enough.

We all have a lot to live for, and there is one thing for certain; we must make the "unseen" crystal clear.

We have to commit to the cause. We must discipline ourselves and disclose the silent killer's tactics. We have to choose to fight for our children and hold everyone accountable for their actions. Parents who are aware and live in denial of their children's actions should be held accountable for those actions. The parents know exactly what is going on, yet they choose not to do anything about it.

We need to dig deep. Higher authorities need to send social workers out to a bully's home to investigate; because something isn't right, and there are so many pieces that are missing from the puzzle. Maybe the children are being abused or neglected at home, and they come to school and take it out on other students and/or teachers.

Yes, enough is enough, but the question is, what is going on in the child's life? The foundation in the bully's home is unmanageable. Something is going on that is clearly being ignored. Questions need to be asked, and answers need to be explained.

These children need help. It isn't fair that our children have to go through the school day in misery. It isn't fair that our children's lives are being turned upside down. It isn't fair that our children isolate themselves from something that they are subjected to.

The children who are bullies need to seek mental help counseling. They need to be tested to see if they have some kind of disability, and if they do, that is okay, but it is only okay if they are treated by a professional.

If the bullies don't have a disability, then their homes need to be evaluated. Maybe they have an aggressive parent, and maybe the child fears their parent. Furthermore, maybe they are suffering from some form of mental, emotional, and physical abuse in the household.

There should be a requirement by law that if constant bullying is occurring, the child needs to be examined to see if help is needed. Bullying starts from somewhere, and wherever that somewhere is it needs to be inspected. The bully needs to be held accountable for the damages they have caused.

If a bullying child needs help, this should not be taken lightly. It should be taken very seriously because their actions destroy lives. If the child doesn't have any issues and continues to bully students and/or teachers, then that child needs to be held accountable, as well as his/her parents. It is hard to feel sympathy for someone who harms your child on purpose.

Parents/guardians, teachers, school administrators, and higher authorities need to be held accountable, and the bully needs to be punished for the consequences of their actions.

Our children who are being bullied shouldn't feel hopeless, they shouldn't fear for their lives, nor should they isolate themselves in silence because someone enjoys causing fear and getting a reaction out of them.

Our babies, regardless of age, should be soaring in the sky like eagles. Their thoughts should be about their desires and imagination. They shouldn't be standing on the edge, hanging by a thread, and breaking down.

Our children should be flying like the wind, and thinking about what they want to change in their lives for the better, whether that is sports, a school subject, a friend, etc. Not being manipulated and thinking about how they are going to change their routine to avoid the bully.

Parents, guardians, teachers, school administrators, and higher authorities, we have to put an end to bullying – and we have to do it now. Our innocent children shouldn't be in the crossfire of their own thoughts just because someone gets a thrill out of it. Enough is enough, and having enough starts today!

CHAPTER 7

Higher Authority

OUR CHILDREN ARE DILIGENT and precious to us. Whether we know it or not, they are fighting an indescribable uphill battle every day. Our children are facing these battles when they are in school because they are dealing with different personalities from their peers, teachers, and administrators. They have a lot of responsibilities, trying to keep up with their coursework, extra activities after school, work (if age appropriate), home, and who knows what else?

They are dealing with peer pressure during school and in the outside world. Sometimes they are fighting a war within themselves because they are trying to find out who they are and where they fit into this world of distractions.

Our children shouldn't lose passion for what they want out of life. Fear shouldn't be our children's first concern due to adversity and complications–that pull them here, there, and everywhere to the point that they lose who they are, who they are trying to be, or want to be in life.

Our children's opportunities should be endless. Unfortunately, the challenges they face at a young age hinder and block their view of every opportunity they missed because their fragile minds were too busy dealing with being in an uncomfortable state.

They aren't only being bullied by their peers; they are bullied by adults as well, whether it's their parents, guardians, teachers, administrators, or higher authorities. Nowadays, children are faced with a lot of challenges and are constantly under pressure.

They need us as adults, regardless of what role we play in their lives, to be understanding, to listen, and to give them an opportunity to express themselves. We, as adults, are too quick to judge and too slow to take accountability for our actions.

My niece is such a loving, smart, and full-of-life little girl. She's always smiling, laughing, and has a huge imagination. My niece is a curious little girl who loves to talk – she wants to know what is this for... why this does that... or why that does this... One of her favorite songs is by Alesia Cara, *How Far I'll Go*. When she sings, she sings the song with so much meaning, and those words come to life. She sings her little heart out because that song means so much to her. My niece is such a joy to be around and she's going to go so far in life.

My niece loves to learn. When she was in preschool, she was number one in her class, as she was in kindergarten through second grade. However, towards the end of her second-grade year, she started to have trouble with one of her teachers. Since there were only a couple of weeks left in school, my sister didn't address the situation. I am a firm believer that some things shouldn't be overlooked; sooner or later it will backfire if it is given enough time to produce flames and explode. When my niece started third grade, the gasoline was put on the flames and it created a wildfire that was out of control.

On the way to lunch, my niece was talking to some of her friends. She noticed her lunchbox felt light and it was slightly unzipped. She walked back into the classroom to get her fruit snacks and apple that she'd left in her cubby. The substitute teacher asked her why she was in the room. She tried explaining that some of her lunch had fallen out of her lunchbox, but he didn't give her time to explain. Instead, he took it upon himself to scream and yell at her.

Quite frankly, she was bullied by her teacher. He took advantage of his position and took it way too far. He took hold of my niece's arm, squeezed it tightly, and pushed her into two desks. My niece feared her teacher as she ran for cover under a desk near the wall. She scooted back as far as she could so he wouldn't be able to grab her. She screamed loudly, "Leave me alone!

Leave me alone! Help!" However, no one came to her rescue, although I'm more than sure someone heard her in the nearby classrooms.

The teacher left my niece in the classroom alone. My niece ate her lunch, shaking in fear under the desk. She didn't come from under the desk until her class came back from lunch.

My niece told my sister what happened and my sister saw the dark red purplish bruise on my niece's arm. My sister took pictures, took her to the emergency room, spoke to the teacher, and principal about what happened – and nothing was done. My sister emailed the school superintendent and sent emails of the pictures as well, yet never received a response.

Had my sister went to the school and attacked the teacher she would have been locked up for disorderly conduct. The substitute teacher should have been locked up for child abuse and fired immediately.

My niece's voice wasn't heard. My sister's actions didn't cause anyone at the Board of Education to blink an eye. They swept her issue under the rug, and it was never brought up again. I never understood why some teachers, principals, administrations, and Boards of Education can turn a blind eye to abuse and bullying in the school system.

Our children shouldn't be tossed around like a Frisbee skimming through the air, being overlooked as if they are invisible. My niece was treated like she didn't exist by her teachers and the Board of Education. Our children do exist, and because they are our babies we have to stand up and fight for them.

We have to fight for our children's rights to be treated as equals and for their voices to be heard. Our babies' mistreatment will not fade into the background. As parents and guardians, we will shed light on what they want to be the "unknown and unseen." It is "known" and it is "crystal clear." The actions of a bully are very familiar and have claimed a place that has shaken up our lives and homes. We will bring forth the truth – it will be front and center because we know lies do not live forever.

Our children will be counted, and justice will be served. Our babies deserve a fair chance at life. We are our children's groundbreakers; therefore, we cannot give up. We might run out of breath but we must have the willpower when moving forward to fight for our children's voices to be heard.

The following school year, my niece encountered another situation at her school, however, it was with a different teacher. A little boy hit my niece in the head with his fist, but while the teacher saw exactly what happened, she continued to teach the class. The little boy hit my niece again, and she screamed "Ouch!" while rubbing her head.

The teacher put my niece out of the classroom. As my niece sat in the hallway, the teacher snatched my niece up by her shirt. She held on to my niece's shirt while she took her down to the lower level of the school (my niece's classroom was on the third floor). One would think, why would a teacher take a child to the lower level of the school? Because there weren't any cameras on the lower level. She took my niece outside to discipline her (as the school system calls it, she "restrained" the student).

The teacher pinned my niece to the wall—put her hands around her neck and choked her until her eyes were bloodshot and red. To make matters worse, my niece has asthma, and the teacher left her outside, gasping for air.

As my niece walked back into the building her classmates asked her why were her eyes red and her shirt wrinkled. My niece told her classmates what happened and she also told a couple of her teachers. However, nobody reported the teacher's behavior. Nobody spoke up.

My sister took pictures, filed a police report and took my niece to the hospital because she had red/purplish bruises around her neck.

My sister went up to the school the very next day. The principal made up tons of excuses about why she couldn't talk to my sister. My sister waited for hours until the principal called her back to her office. The principal called the teacher who choked my niece to her office as well, but during the meeting, the teacher sat in silence. She didn't answer my sister's questions, nor did she deny what happened.

The principal asked my sister for the pictures. She looked them over and sent the teacher back to class. The teacher wasn't suspended or fired. The principal neglected to ask the other teachers who were aware of what happened to come to the office. To sum it up, the principal didn't care.

Later that evening, my sister received a call from the principal. The principal said my niece was being disrespectful in class, therefore, the teacher had the right to restrain the student if he/she was out of line.

My sister was furious and asked the principal to produce the tape of the incident. She went on to say, "The teacher didn't have the right to take my daughter to the basement away from the camera, take her outside, pin her on the wall, choke her, and leave her there, gasping for air."

The principal told my sister she couldn't produce the tape. My sister used social media as her voice; she posted what happened on the media. She also contacted the local news station and a lawyer.

The next day, the principal pulled my niece out of class without my sister knowing. An investigator and social worker interrogated and recorded my niece's version about what had happened. They tried to convince my niece that nothing had happened. They tried to manipulate my niece but she told the truth without fear. My sister was livid. They also had a social worker come out to the house to investigate the household, which didn't make sense because the abuse happened at the school, not at home.

My niece was being interrogated, my sister's home was being investigated, and the social worker was involved for months. My sister's home was violated. The school asked the investigator and social worker to make sure there weren't any drugs or violent abuse in the home. The situation got out of hand, and my sister's attorney wasn't happy with all of the false allegations the school tried to place on my niece and sister.

The Board of Education never questioned the teachers. They went on every day as if nothing ever happened. The teachers weren't suspended while the investigation was taking place; they were being protected by the Board for their wrongdoing. The teachers knew they could get away with it because they were immune to accusations of bullying and putting hands on their students.

As parents and guardians, we have to question the higher authority. Clearly, there is a huge problem with this picture. How could blame be placed on the students and parents for the teacher's disorderly conduct?

My sister contacted the Board of Education daily by phone, fax, and email. They took down her name and number but nobody never called or emailed her back.

Sadly, nearly a year passed by and the teacher was never investigated by the school system. The fingers were pointed at my niece, a little eight-year-old who was in the third grade. Shame on the school system.

Some educators abuse their power to the fullest and in an unhealthy way. The question that needs to be asked is, who will protect our children? As parents and guardians, we send our children off to school to get an education with hopes they will return to us alive and well.

My niece was afraid to go to school. It was one thing after another. My niece's teacher would roll her eyes at my niece as she walked down the hall.

One of the teachers pulled her out of class and called her all kinds of names. She got in my niece's face and started to yell and scream at her for no reason. My niece closed her eyes and put her hands over her ears and started to hum. The teacher yelled, "Look at me, you little bitch. You are going to listen to me." She pulled my niece's hands down. My niece screamed really loud, "Leave me alone. Shut up. Leave me alone. Stop picking on me. Leave me alone."

After all of that, I am more than sure someone heard the teacher and my niece, but nobody came to her rescue.

The teachers verbally abused my niece and nothing was done. They physically abused her and again, nothing was done. Clearly, they crossed the line of basic discipline. They constantly tortured my niece by bullying her, being manipulative, and humiliating her. Her teachers let other students bully her as well without a care. What a horrible thing to do to a child.

How can all of that go unheard, ignored, and sidetracked? How is that possible?

After my sister's post on social media about what happened to my niece, there were parents contacting my sister, and they recognized my sister in the neighborhood. Parents were coming from all over saying the same teachers bullied their children as well.

Some teachers bully students on a daily basis and do not have a care in the world because they know they will not have to face any consequences. It is impossible to believe but it is true. They "think" they are covered by the system, and they know they can get away with it.

The system is corrupt and it needs to change, and it needs to improve for the better of our children, the students. A couple of weeks ago, a teacher was suspended for telling her students to turn their shirts inside out. The principal suspended the teacher while the investigation took place. There were parents protesting; they wanted the teacher to be fired. Two weeks later, the teacher resigned.

Something is seriously wrong with this picture. Parents can protest because a teacher asked her students to turn their shirt inside out, and the principal and the Board can suspend the teacher but teachers who put hands on innocent children are not held accountable for their actions.

The Board of Education listened to the parents who were protesting because of an issue with a t-shirt, but parents are ignored when our children are being abused by the educators. This is ridiculously crazy. Needless to say, the teacher quit because her life was being threatened. Why didn't the Board of Education protect the teacher? They protect the teachers when they abuse the students.

There are some teachers who are bullied and abused by the students, higher authorities, and parents as well, but sadly, nothing is said.

My oldest son had an outstanding Spanish teacher in high school. He was very much involved in the school. He was the tennis coach, a mentor to the students, and he always put his best foot forward. When the tennis team didn't have the proper equipment and uniforms, he set up a Go Fund Me account to raise money (he raised enough to get the team new equipment and uniforms). He and his parents donated money to the tennis team as well. After each game, he would take the team to get pizza (which he paid for out of his own pocket).

He was my son's mentor, and until this day he is family.

My son called me, very disturbed because a student tried to jump his Spanish teacher. The student broke the teacher's laptop, threw books at him, turned over all the desks, and ripped pictures off the wall. All because the teacher took the student's phone.

The teacher had to leave the school grounds until the higher authority investigated the situation. When he walked to his car, he saw that his windows were busted and his tires were slashed.

What made matters worse, the student's parent came up to the school, complaining and making a fuss over the child's phone being taken away. Wow! I was speechless. What is going on in the world today? The parent wasn't concerned about what the child had done; she was focused on getting the child's phone back.

After the case was completed, the teacher had an option to either resign or be fired. I was highly disappointed at how the principal and Board of Education handled this serious problem.

The student should have been kicked out of school and the student's parents should have been held accountable for the teacher's broken laptop and for the damage done to the teacher's car.

He was one of the few teachers at the school who cared for his student's well-being. He was focused on the student's education, and he wanted to make sure the students had activities to choose from as opposed to just the basics. This was a serious problem and justice wasn't served on his behalf.

I understand there is a chain of command to follow. However, when will justice be served after the parent, guardian and/or teacher has followed the chain of command? When the problem reaches the higher authority, it never surprises me at how many excuses are always given, and/or the issues are covered up with a lie. It is very rare that the parents, guardians, or teacher's voices are heard in regards to speaking up for the children or themselves.

What is the purpose of a "chain of command" when the higher authorities don't follow the rules and regulations that they made? Are the higher authorities entitled to break the rules? Is it fair that they have known of the issue for some time? However, sadly, the issues are never resolved. Yet it is covered up by manipulating the student, teachers, and/or parent. If it's being covered up, when and how will our voices be heard?

The chain of command consists of people who start from a lower level such as a teacher. They then progress to a senior teacher, head of teacher development, vice-principal, principal, principal supervisor, superintendent and so on. However, before they work their way up the ladder, if the issue hasn't been resolved there will be a teacher, parent, and principal conference. If that doesn't work either, that is when the Board of Educator's Administrators becomes involved.

When it reaches the Board of Education, clearly, they are familiar with the issue at hand, yet the issue is pushed to the side. They look at it as if it is not their problem. That is where the issue lies...

I have a friend who is a teacher. I am always surprised when I hear what he has to deal within the school system. We must not forget there are some teachers who have our children's best interests at heart. However, it is hard for them to step up and speak out because they are afraid to put their jobs on the line, and because they have to care for their families. Therefore, they are faced with a dilemma: whether to either speak up for what is right, damage their name and lose it all, or keep quiet and let the mistreatment continue.

My son called me because he was having an asthma attack and the nurse had told him to put a wet paper towel over his nose and mouth. My son asked her if he could go to his locker to retrieve his medication. She yelled at my son and said, "You are a stupid boy! I am a nurse I know more than you about asthma, and you need to sit your ass right here and do what I say!"

When I walked into the building to check my son out of school to take him to the hospital, he was sitting in the front office with a wet paper towel on his face, breathing so hard to the point I could see his rib cage through his shirt. When I checked him out of school the front desk clerk told my son he would have to go downstairs to get a pass to be released. Clearly, she didn't wake up with her brain in her skull that particular morning. I had some words for her as my son and I walked out to go to the ER.

The physician told me my son was in the red zone and we were lucky that we arrived when we did or my son would have died.

The very next day, I went to the school. I had some words for the nurse, and you better believe I wrote to the Board of Education; I wasn't surprised when I didn't hear anything back. However, that didn't stop me. I contacted the Board of Nursing, submitted my document of proof along with the physician's statement to make sure the nurse's license was terminated. I had to put up a fight, but I won. I didn't want anyone's life to be in her hands. My son almost died because of her negligent behavior.

My daughter called me and asked me if I could pick her up from school because she'd been suspended. It wasn't April, so I knew it wasn't an April fool's joke. I asked her, "Where is your teacher, assistant principal, principal, ugh someone?" I asked because I'd never heard of a student calling to say they were suspended. I thought that was an educator's or a school administrator's responsibility.

The assistant principal got on the phone and said, "Hi, Ms. Jackson, Sarah is suspended because she kicked a young man in his private parts." I was shocked because my daughter wouldn't purposely hit anyone. I asked, "What did he do to her?" because I know my daughter wouldn't start a fight "just because."

The assistant principal said, "Well, there was a group of people who were in a crowd and we saw Sarah's puffball (her hair was in a ball) on the camera."

As I was talking to the assistant principal on the phone I was on my way to the school. I said, "Puffball? There are a lot of students who put their hair in a bow that forms a puffball."

She replied, "It looked like Sarah."

I quoted her and said, "Looked like?"

I walked into the building and I asked Sarah what happened. She explained she was walking to class, the guy was standing against the wall, and he tripped her. She dropped her books, fell hard on her knees, got up, and roundhouse kicked the young man in the privates.

I replied, "Sarah, you did a good job defending yourself."

The teachers and assistant principal looked at me and said, "Ms. Jackson, a young man is in pain."

I replied, "As he should be! If he would have kept his foot on the ground, he wouldn't be in the shape he's in. I am going to stand by what I said, and he deserved exactly what he got. He has everyone's sympathy because he bent down to hold his private parts. You should know that Sarah was supposed to knee him in the face as well. She's in Tae Kwon Do, and that's how we are supposed to finish our attacker."

I then asked, "Was the young man suspended too?"

I was told no because his private parts were injured.

Of course, I was upset – and they didn't hear the last of me.

I tried talking to the principal about the situation. She had the nerve to ignore me as she sorted out the letters to put on the announcement board. Finally, she said, without making eye contact, "I do not know what happened."

I firmly said, "Aren't you the head of the school?"

She kept her eyes on the letters and said, "Yes, I am. That's me."

I looked at her and said, "Since you are the head of the school, you're supposed to know every incident that happens at your school. Instead, you are too busy being sarcastic when someone asks you a question." I had to let her know that I wasn't a parent to be taken lightly. Respectfully, I broke down the definition of a leader and made her aware that she didn't fit the description. I explained to her that not all people are meant to lead; some are meant to follow because they cannot handle the task of leadership.

This was the same principal who never responded to my emails when I had an issue with one of Sarah's teacher. However, she emailed me tons of times and asked Sarah multiple times if she was going on a field trip. I couldn't believe she even asked me that but neglected to respond to an important matter. I used her actions as a perfect example as I explained to her that she didn't have the qualifications to be a leader. Nowadays, education isn't taken seriously.

Sarah was suspended for two days and the young man wasn't expelled. After I spoke my piece, I was fine because we treated her suspension as if we were on a mini-vacation. We had a Mommy and Sarah day, we went to the movies, out to eat, and had a good time.

And you'd better believe I told Sarah, her teacher, assistant principal, the principal, and the administrators, "If someone attacks my daughter, please know she will defend herself."

I never understood why innocent children are punished for defending themselves when the troubled students started it. I pondered on it for a day or two, then I realized – the innocent children are punished or suspended because they are the ones who respect the teachers. The teachers want to make an example of the good students to make it seem like they are strict and have things under control.

However, when the students who make trouble are disrespectful, they never say anything to them because they are scared of those students. They know those students will talk or fight back. Furthermore, they know most of the time the trouble-making students' parents will go up to the school raising hell. They make an example of the respectful students because they know they will listen and abide by the rules.

When it comes to the Board of Education, our children, the parents, guardians, and some teachers are on a carousel going around and around without seeing results. It's so bad nowadays, that the Board doesn't procrastinate anymore; their actions are boldly giving the message that they do not care.

They use their resources to cover up the truth. Their words speak of a lack of clarity by stirring up the pot with no purpose because they produce one lie after another until they start to believe it. They feel as though they do not have to justify their actions, yet they feel like they have the right to interrogate our children who are vulnerable and paralyzed by the fear they put in their minds.

As parents, guardians, and teachers who are being treated unfairly, we have to be productive, regardless of all the chaos. We cannot be passive, and we have to lay the foundation of truth, the foundation of justice, and the foundation of ownership to obtain closure once and for all to the silent killers that we call bullies.

Take Time to Listen

PARENTS AND GUARDIANS HAVE to be more involved in their children's life. I hear this phrase often, and sometimes I am a victim of the saying, "Time is never on my side. There isn't enough time in a day. If only I had more time."

As parents and guardians, we have so many things to do in a day. Time slips through our fingers and passes us by without us noticing what we accomplished during the day. Most of the time, the only things that run through our minds are the things we haven't completed. We squeeze in what needs to be done and try to compete with time to make sure everything is done before time expires for the day.

I am a firm believer that "time is everything." Sometimes "time" can make things difficult. However, it gives us the ability to analyze; define transition and reexamine our lives. Despite the outcome of the situation, "time" is rewarding because when all is said and done, it works out in our favor.

Time is an observer, it reminds me of a microscope because it magnifies within time what we cannot see with the naked eye. Time is a natural connection – it reveals and helps us clarify what was overlooked and what we didn't understand. Time can be a 'Catch-22' because it can be unreasonable, selfish, challenging, frightening, vulnerable, and cut-throat. However, time isn't meant to stay the same; therefore, time changes. Once time has moved on, you cannot get that moment back.

Which brings me to the fact that time is fragile, precious, and sensitive. We need to make time for our children. Time is of the essence in all things, it ticks with each breath. Within the blink of an eye, our children, who were once someone we could cradle in our arms, are now young adults, because time took its course.

Time is persistent, and we need to make the best of it.

I am not perfect, but one thing's for sure, I always make time for my children. My children and I have a bond that is unbreakable. We are not perfect. We have our ups and downs, and at times, we know how to agree to disagree. However, as a parent, I know when to give my children space. Giving our children a little lead way and space is very important because our children have to make their own mistakes and learn from them.

As a parent, I know when to be the "strict" parent. There are times when what I say goes, and there will be no questions asked. I am the parent, and whatever the situation may be at that given time, as the parent, I see and know the outcome because I've been there and done that before.

As I stated before, our children need to live and learn from their own mistakes but when a huge mistake could possibly be prevented, why not as the parent try to steer our children in another direction? That "huge" mistake could destroy our children's lives–something that is possibly not too easy to come back from.

Although my children and I have open communication, at times I give them space. I ask questions, and I try to understand their point of view. However, I do have rules and regulations in my household. When my children find themselves in a mess, most of the time I give them the benefit of the doubt by listening, but you better believe it, foremost in their minds they know they will reap what they sowed.

First, I lecture them about their actions. Secondly, after I talk to them, I then let them explain to me what they could have done differently to change the situation. Thirdly, I let them explain to me and clarify why they are being disciplined. The reason why I let them do this is because I want them to hear themselves speaking out loud regarding what they said or did, and most of the time, they'll say, "Mom, what I did was so stupid. I do not understand why I did that." Lastly, I discipline my children depending on how much damage they caused.

We have to realize we are our children's parents and guardians. We shouldn't cover up their wrongdoing. We shouldn't make excuses for our children because if we do, we are causing more harm than good. We shouldn't think twice about disciplining our children. When we cover up and support our children in their wrongdoing without having them face the consequences, we are not serving them any justice. Instead, we are weakening and damaging our children.

As parents and guardians, we want to protect our children but we have to teach our children that there are repercussion in life caused by the choices and the decisions they make.

However, we must lead by example as well. There are times when I am in the wrong and as a parent, I have to take ownership and apologize. When I was a little girl, I was told a parent shouldn't apologize to their child. I never understood why.

As for me, in my household, we have family discussions on what we all can do better. There are times when my children voice their opinions in a respectful manner and tell me how they feel. If I take something way too far by my actions or words, they explain it to me. I then ponder over it maybe during the meeting and/or over a day or two, and if I feel like I was in the wrong I will apologize to my children for my faults.

As parents and guardians, we aren't perfect. We make mistakes too, and we are not always right. Our children have opinions, and I feel like they should be able to express themselves in a respectful way. In my household, my children have a voice, and they know they can express their feelings – but in a respectful manner. When I was young, my daddy always used to tell my siblings and me to remember that as children we have a voice as well and we need to know how and when to use it by speaking up in a respectful way. That built confidence within my siblings and me.

As parents and guardians, we have our shortcomings as well, but all of them are lessons to be learned, and it builds confidence within ourselves and our children. It opens up doors and windows of unconditional love, determination, courage, trust, balance, overcoming challenges, and so much more. Most importantly, it builds a phenomenal relationship with our children.

I will admit I am human; therefore, I am guilty of being in my feelings; of not hearing my children out at times when I ask them to do something over and over again; it's either done incorrectly or they never complete the task because they forget.

I am also guilty of not hearing my children out when I ask them not to do something, whether it's at home, school, at a friend's house, etc., and they do it anyway and find themselves in a world of trouble.

What makes it far worse is that as the parent, and by them being my responsibility by law, even in their teenage stages, I am liable for some of their actions. This means a parent has to step up to handle the situation they've put themselves in. It takes a toll on me because I told them not to participate in what they did. It takes up more of my time that I do not have, or if I did have the time, it would have been for something more useful.

I am not a perfect parent but when my children have a problem, they know they are always welcome to talk to me. If I see something that isn't right by the tone in their voice, their appearance – whether it be physical or emotional – I ask questions.

There are times when they have a snappy attitude, but believe me, their attitude does not steer me away from asking questions. If we do not ask, we will never know. Also, asking questions lets our children know we are concerned. They will see we care, and that opens up a line of communication and trust.

We must have a relationship with our children. I notice there isn't a lot of love going around in some families; and most definitely not enough hugs and kisses given to our children.

Every day, before my children and I start our day, we make sure we tell each other to have a great day, we give each other a hug, blow kisses, and tell each other we love each other.

During dinner, we ask how each other's day was; and before going to bed we give each other a hug, kiss, and we tell each other, I love you. I carried this along to my children because this was my upbringing with my mom and daddy.

Our children want to feel love and comfort. It's never too late to love on our children. The world is full of cold, distasteful, cruel, and manipulative people. By having a relationship with our children, we are laying out the foundation of trust, open arms, communication, possibilities, and confidence.

We, as the parents and guardians, are our children's first chance in life. We are the first people who give our children a fair chance. We form bonds with our children by having a relationship with them, and as time passes and they grow older, they will know they are always more than welcome to talk to their parents and guardians.

Even if a parent has never had a relationship with their child, it is never too late to talk to them, be more involved in their life and well-being, confess your mistakes, and start working on your relationship. They will be more willing to talk to you and disclose slowly but surely what's going on in their life.

When we have a relationship with our children, little do we know we are building confidence from within to make them want to shoot for the stars. As they grow, they are becoming wiser, and oftentimes the road they travel in their childhood years until the present and near-future are all the things that were taught by us having a good relationship with them. It will pay off in the long run because they have paid attention and listened to what was said from their parents and guardians. Sometimes we may think that it falls on deaf ears, but most of the time they are listening.

My oldest son was in a disagreement with one of his teachers, and his teacher kicked him out of the class. My son came home and talked to me about what happened. I listened and told my son, both of them were in the wrong because neither of them would listen to each other.

I went to talk to the teacher. However, as I was walking down the hallway, I saw the teacher was in my son's face and yelling at him. He was telling my son he was not allowed to come in his classroom, and he asked another teacher to let my son sit in his classroom.

The advisor who walked me down to the classroom didn't know what to do or say. When I begin to talk, the advisor wanted to step in and say, please step aside and let me handle it. I told him, "You had your time to step in, but you froze."

I walked up to my son and his teacher. His teacher said, "Little girl, go back to class. This doesn't have anything to do with you."

I said, "I beg your pardon, I am not a student, I am Xavier's mother."

He looked at me and said, "I do not care if you are his mother, your son will not be sitting in my class."

I look at him with a straight face, and in a firm voice, I said, "Sir, your class has already started and your students are waiting for you to teach. How about I sit in the class with my son, and after class, we can discuss the problem?" He agreed.

After class, we sat down and talked about the problem. When all was said and done, neither the teacher nor Xavier wanted to hear each other out. I told Xavier he should have respected the teacher's rules. I made sure Xavier had an understanding of his actions. I told him he was too old not respect the rules and regulations of the classroom – and he knows better. I told him he was most definitely wrong for bringing snacks in the class after the teacher asked him not to.

I told the teacher, "Sometimes we have to be mindful of how we talk to people. Xavier is in tenth grade, and these kids think they know everything. However, when I was a young girl, I was always taught that to get respect you have to earn it, and vice versa. I was always taught, everyone deserves respect. Xavier was wrong, but you came at him wrong as well. The problem escalated when both of you were talking over each other."

I went on to say, "I believe you should apologize to each other." Xavier and his teacher heard each other out and apologized. His teacher said, "Ms. Jackson, we need more parents like you because I didn't think the conversation would end up this way. Most of the time, parents come in cursing out the teachers but I've never had a parent come to sit down and speak with so much knowledge to both the teacher and student."

I replied, "My daddy always taught us that everyone should respect each other and that communication is the key."

I made sure they understood the term "communication." People think communication is a form of going back and forth. However, that's only part of what the term means. I think people are confused because going back and forth is a big part of communicating (there are pros and cons), therefore, in order to break down the term "communication" one must understand the term "listening" which is very crucial in solving an issue.

Another term that is important is "understanding." Which, is the foundation of the term "communication." Furthermore, if you put listening and understanding together that is 90% of communication. Going back and forth is only 10% of communication. If one doesn't listen or understand, going back and forth is irrelevant. We can go back and forth and speak over each other; but the big question is, are we listening and understanding what the other person is saying?

The definition of communication is listening and understanding. Sometimes that term extends its unselfish ways; by asking for that person to consider what was asked during the conversation. Meaning, sometimes when we listen and understand what was asked while talking back and forth, we have to think about what was said.

We have to take time to listen and understand but maybe an answer isn't given at that particular time—and it is okay to say, "I do not know" or "I do not have an answer, but I will ask someone who knows," etc. It is okay because we do not have all of the answers and we do not know all of the answers.

We are supposed to come together, listen, understand, and help each other. Not everyone is meant to lead. However, I've noticed that everyone wants to lead, but nobody wants to listen to each other.

After our conversation, Xavier and his teacher got along and he ended tenth grade on a good note. We have to let our children know that we will be there for them when the situation becomes impossible for them to handle. With that being said, we have to be honest and let them know when they are wrong as well. We have to advocate for our children; that also builds trust, hope, and confidence within our children.

Elijah came home one day and said he didn't like going to school anymore. I was quick to ask if he was being bullied again (that was the first thing that came to mind). He responded "No, school is too hard. I never get the answers right in math." I felt bad because Elijah is such a hard worker. Every day, he comes home to start on his homework immediately. For a fourth-grader, he is very responsible. He would say, "Mom, I can't go to soccer practice today or Tae Kwon Do because I have a lot of homework to do. I need time to complete it and I do not want to get behind."

I was concerned. His teachers were kind enough to meet with Elijah and me. Elijah expressed his feelings. I did too, and his teachers expressed their feelings as well. His teachers were beyond phenomenal. They went over Elijah's work and showed him how well he was doing. They made it clear to him that he's where he needs to be. However, we all need to take a break from time to time.

His fourth grade teachers were awesome and I love them dearly. I must say, the teachers at his school go above and beyond when it comes to educating their students. When a parent has a concern or two, they always make time to be there to listen and to help solve the problem. They are amazing teachers and I truly appreciate them.

After the meeting, Elijah walked out with confidence and a better understanding of knowing when he is putting too much pressure on himself.

As parents and guardians, we must take time out to listen to our children. We cannot push their needs to the side or procrastinate; we must attend to their needs immediately. When our children express their needs, we have to set a tone of how we respond to them. We can either ignore their needs and make our children feel like they do not matter, or we can listen and take action on their needs and let them know they are important to us.

By catering to their needs, we are transforming our children to think in a positive way. We are teaching them that obstacles can be conquered. We are showing them by our actions that they have the right to justify their words and actions. As we listen to their needs, they are seeing that their voices are being heard. As we acknowledge their needs, we are teaching them not to settle for "whatever" or "it is what it is." We are teaching them that there is always an answer to a question and a solution to a problem.

Willingness to show we are interested in our children's needs takes the burden and worries off their minds. It shows compassion on our end, and it builds trust on their end. As a single mother, I consider it a privilege that my children trust me enough to come and talk to me about what is going on in their lives.

I learned that the little things matter. When my children were smaller, I put encouraging letters in their lunch boxes, I read to them as I held them in my arms until they fell asleep. I gave, and still, until this day, give them dozens of hugs a day, and sometimes I act silly and dance with them.

We always spend family time together, whether it is a movie night or one-on-one time with them individually. I discipline them, make eye contact whether they are right or wrong, and tell them I love them on a daily basis. I make sure I recognize them, whether for good or bad. I reward them (sometimes) for the good, they have done. I try my best to keep my promises. We go for walks in the park, we reminisce, laugh, and learn so much about each other. Ha! As you know, children change what they like and dislike on a daily basis, therefore, we are learning something new about them every day!

Honestly, spending time with my children brings the child out in me. Sometimes I forget about my worries, stressful life, and responsibilities just for the moment. I am at peace, and the best medicine, which is laughter, suddenly cures my hectic life. It relaxes me and brings my children and me closer together. They are a bundle of joy and I couldn't ask for better!

It's the smallest things that form a relationship and trust with our children. As parents and guardians, we are not perfect by far, but if we give our children unconditional love, listen, and be there during the good and bad, I'm sure our children will appreciate it and see we want the best for them at all times, and by any means necessary.

CHAPTER 9

What About Us?

WE NEED TO OPEN our eyes and see bullying for what it is. The silent killer is stirring the pot, manipulating our children, and stealing their innocence. Some of our children have given in to the fight but there is no reason why our children should submit to physical harm, verbal abuse, and being tortured for no reason.

As parents, guardians, teachers, school administrators, and higher authorities, we have to tear down the wall of bullying. We have to hold the silent killer responsible for its actions. We are a powerful force and if we all can come together, we will put an end to the silent killer once and for all.

The children of the world today are speaking up, but some of us aren't listening. Here are some of our children's anonymous testimonies of what they go through on a daily basis:

~~~

"I do not like recess. Instead, I ask my teacher if I can have a library pass. For the past couple of days, she would say no. I told her I do not like recess because my classmates pick on me. She looked at me as if she didn't believe me. She insisted that I play with my "friends." I told her I do not have any friends. The way she looked at me; it was like she was saying to herself, I do not have time for this little drama. I had no choice but to go to recess. I kicked the ball around by myself.

A couple of my classmates made it look like they were playing kickball with me—which they weren't. They kept throwing the ball at me and calling me names. I went over to tell the teacher, and she told me to play with someone else. I sat on the bench and waited until recess was over. The boys came over and poured red dirt in my hair.

One of the guys punched me in the nose and it started to bleed. He punched me again. This time he punched me in my mouth and it started to bleed as well. I tried to get up and tell the teacher but they blocked me in and told me if I told I would get a beat down. I cleaned my face with my t-shirt that was under my sweater.

I wasn't going to let them tell me what to do so I told the teacher, who gave me a pass to go to the nurse. Sad to say, the teacher didn't punish the boys.

When I went to lunch, the boys took my lunch tray and threw my food in the trash. They opened the milk carton and said my hair was too dirty and it needed to be washed. They poured the milk on my head. They said, "We told you we were going to beat you; instead we are going to make your life a living hell."

I talked to another teacher and asked him what I was supposed to do. He told me to tell my parents. My parents fought for me but the boys never got suspended. My mom transferred me to another school. Why is it that bad people get away with everything? What about the good kids. What about me?"

~ ~ ~

"For no reason, I was slapped in the face in the middle of the hallway. My classmates would throw things at me in class – pens, pencils, balled-up paper, and call me all kinds of names when the teacher left the room. However, when the teacher returned, everyone acted as nothing happened. What I didn't understand was why the teacher didn't say anything about all the pens, paper, and pencils on the floor? I feel like teachers don't ask because they do not want to know.

From time to time, I was kicked in the private area for no reason; just because they knew they could get away with it. Most of the time, my teachers see everything, but it is ignored.

Every day, I felt useless. I went home and cut off my hair and took an overdose of pills. Next thing I knew, I was in the hospital on suicide watch. All I could think of was, why did they save me? I wanted to die. When my parents dropped me off at school, I would skip school every day. My grades dropped, but I didn't care. All I could do was watch my back and think about me."

~~~

"I was slammed into my locker today and kicked directly in the stomach for being overweight. I am trying to lose weight, but it is hard. I starve myself, but that is not good enough. When I eat something, I like, I love the taste of it, but I will vomit it up so I will not gain weight. I look at all the pretty and skinny girls and ask myself, why can't I be pretty? Why can't I be small and petite? When I look in the mirror, I hate the person who is looking back at me. The girls at my school do not make it any better. I'm not allowed to sit at anyone's table during lunch.

They say, "It looks like you ate more than enough fat stuff." They call me all kinds of names to make me feel worse about myself. One day, I purposely took more than ten diet pills in the girl's restroom, then I sat in the corner behind the door. A teacher found me with foam coming out of my mouth. I was rushed to the hospital. The doctor advised my parents to put me into a psychiatric hospital because this had happened more than one time. It is not my fault. I try to love myself, but when I go to school my self-esteem is shot down by my classmates. I tried explaining to my parents and the doctor, but they think I have a mental disability. I begged and pleaded, What about me?"

~~~

"I cry myself to sleep every night. I feel like nobody cares. I talked to my teachers, principal, and parents about the bullying at school. It goes in one ear and out the other. My life doesn't matter. Why am I here?

My weight goes up and down due to stress from my peers. I have social anxiety because my voice is never heard. When I try to speak up, people shut me down left and right. I try to tell my parents about my day in school but they are too busy. People think I am a weirdo because I listen to rock music. They think I worship the devil because I wear black, but black is my favorite color. They call me the devil's child because of my high boots, dark-colored hair, and piercings.

My parents are so attached to their professional careers I feel like I was a mistake. Nobody fights for me. I do not have anybody to turn to or talk to. Only my music. Some days, I just want to die. I don't know how I am going to get through life.

I just want to be heard. I want someone to love me and listen to me. I want to be loved more than ever. I am tired of being mistreated and called black sheep. Why do I have to go through this? What about me, Mom and Dad? What about me?"

~ ~ ~

"I think going to school is a nightmare. My classmates pick on me because of my accent. I cannot help that, I am from another country. I talk to my teachers but they ignore me. They act like they do not understand what I am saying. I spoke with the assistant principal and principal about it and they brushed it off. I want to go back to live in my country. Why do I have to be here? I am so lonely. I do not have any friends. I hate being here. What about me and my feelings?"

~ ~ ~

"I never feel at ease when walking into the school building. My classmates are always whispering, staring, and talking about me. One day, my phone kept vibrating in class; I looked down and it was a picture of my face next to a hippopotamus. Next thing I knew, everyone who had a phone received the picture. How am I supposed to go on throughout my day? My heart hurts, my head hurts, and I feel sick.

I am scared to go to the restroom because I am more than sure everyone who has a phone has the picture. What am I supposed to do? My mind is running a thousand miles per hour. My classroom is on the fifth floor. The only way out is jumping out the window. Should I jump or walk into a disaster? What about me?"

~ ~ ~

"I have a learning disability called Autism. People make fun of me because of my social skills, and most times it is very challenging for me to communicate because I stutter a lot as well. I try my best to talk at a steady pace but I cannot move as fast as the other kids. They called me a parrot because most of the time I have to repeat after my teacher in order to have an understanding.

My teachers tell the students to be respectful but they never listen. My classmates call me stupid and an ignorant fool because I am not capable of learning fast. I try not to let it bother me, but it does. I try to keep a positive attitude, but when I am alone, I cry. I think about taking my life on a daily basis because I do not want to live. I hate who I am. What about me?"

~ ~ ~

"I have to put up a fight every day when I go to school. The same boys take my lunch money. I always fight back, but I always lose. They would push me down on the floor, take off my shoes, and take my lunch money out of my socks. I used to put my money in my back pants pocket, but it was too easy for them. I tried to be creative and hid the money in my socks, but I guess I wasn't creative enough. One of the guys told me I better not hide them anywhere else or they would take off my clothes and I would walk around the school naked. This place is horrible. I tell my teachers but they never do anything about it. I am so embarrassed to tell my parents. I have no choice because this is getting out of hand. When I walk home from school, I take the long way home to think. I ask myself, what is my purpose in life? What about me?"

~ ~ ~

"Why do I call my friends my "friends?" I feel like a "stand-by" person when it is beneficial for them. They treat me like the oddball. They don't let me in on their secrets, I never know why they are laughing. At times, they cut their eyes at me and I can't help but think they are talking about me. I know it is my fault; I am making a dumb decision to hang out with them.

When I tried to part ways, they made my life miserable. Someone put sticky honey in my locker with a note saying I can't ever leave the group unless I am given permission. There were times when they played mind games with me; they would tell me when I can sit with the "crew" during lunch.

Most days, I sit at the table, but when I do, I am better off having lunch alone because they treat me like I don't exist. I was told by one of the girls that I am nobody but their extra sidekick. They treat me so badly. I can't speak up. If I do, I will make the situation worse. If I talk to someone, who knows what might happen? I am going to have to deal with it until the end of the school year.

I walk the halls looking happy but on the inside I am miserable. I tell myself all the time I deserve better. When I look at my reflection, I am not happy with myself, I am ashamed because I feel powerless. I have to ask myself often, what about me? Don't I deserve better? I answer, I do, but how do I get out?"

~~~

"Charity case, loner, black sheep, little mutt, bulldog face. Those are some of the names I am called by my peers. The bullying became so bad I began cutting myself. It got to the point the pain numbed my feelings. I would cut myself on my arms, legs, stomach, hips, the side of my back, and sometimes I could prick my fingers with a thumbtack, staples, or a paper clip.

I never understood why I would ever hurt myself, knowing other people hurt me too. I love myself, but maybe not enough. Bullying takes a toll on a person, both mentally and physically. I am so tired of being treated so badly. The bullying has gone on for so long I do not know how to stand up for myself. In my mind, I do not matter. In my mind, I am a failure. In my mind, I am invisible. What about me? I think to myself over and over again. That is a good question, but I never have an answer."

~ ~ ~

"I tried to hang myself but I didn't have the courage to jump off the step. My mother's face kept coming to mind. She is the reason why I couldn't jump. I do not want to hurt my mother. I do not know if there's an afterlife, but if there is, I do not want to look down on my mom and see her in pain because of my selfish ways. I am so tired of reading my chat messages; they would say:

"Kill yourself."

"You're not wanted or loved."

"Jump off a cliff."

"Why haven't you did yourself off already?"

"Ugh, you woke up this morning."

"Do yourself a favor and dive off a building."

"Die. Die. Die."

"The world is a horrible place because you are in it."

"You are useless."

Cyberbullying is real. I should delete my social media accounts or cut off my phone and/or laptop, but I am always curious. Sometimes I believe things will get better, and they would forget about me and things would die down, but everything seems like it's getting worse. Cyberbullying is destroying my life. How could people be so cruel? Help me. Save me. Why me? What about me?"

~ ~ ~

"They say I am hopeless and that I do not matter. They call me a loser and stupid. How is that when I am the smartest person in the class? They say my mother doesn't love or care about me. I know that is not true, but they can be so convincing. Who in their right mind wants to live like this every day? I tell myself, yesterday is the past and today is another day of misery. It seems like every day repeats itself. I ask myself every single day, what is it about me they do not like?"

~ ~ ~

"When I raise my hand in class my classmates say I think I am better than them because I know the answer. That isn't true. I do my homework and study every day during lunch and after school. Maybe they should do the same. I hate going to the restroom; most of the time I hold it until I get home.

The last time, I used the restroom the "popular" girls pushed me around. They filled a bottle up with toilet water and poured it on me. I didn't have a change of clothes so I went to the Lost and Found, but there weren't any clothes that fit me. I told my teacher what happened. She acted like she didn't care. My principal is never around.

I walked around until my clothes dried. Life sucks. I walked around all day thinking and saying over and over again, I have feelings. I am a person. I am a human being. I couldn't help but think, "What about me?"

~ ~ ~

"I didn't know how to pronounce my teacher's name. When I asked her how to pronounce her name, she told me to get out of her class. I was taken aback because I asked a simple question. I asked again, and she called security on me. The officer came into the classroom, jerked me out from my desk, slammed me on the floor and put his knee on my back while he put cuffs on me.

I hate coming to this school. It is more like a prison because they treat students like inmates. If it's not the teachers bullying the students, it's the students bullying each other to seem like they are cool so they will not be bullied themselves. When I was on the ground being tortured. I asked the officer, "What about me? Are you going to ask me what happened?" He told me to shut up as he dragged me out of the room and down the hallway. I yelled as he was pushing me around, "WHAT ABOUT ME?"

~ ~ ~

"Cyberbullying turned my life upside down. I do not know why I continued to read what was said about me in the group chat but I wanted to know what people thought about me. I was teased because I had an overbite and a lazy eye. I was called cockeyed and a woodpecker. It didn't make it any better that I was a tomboy.

One day, when I was on the bus, a girl hit me with her backpack so hard it knocked me unconscious. Nobody knew I was left on the bus. When I awoke, I had a bad headache and I was on the school bus, lying on the seat. I guess the driver neglected to check her seats to make sure everyone was off. The bus was parked in a parking lot. I didn't see an address so I stayed on the bus until the bus driver returned and drove to the school for the afternoon pick up.

I spoke to my mom about it, and she was furious but the administrators didn't care. It went in one ear and out the other. They made up excuses saying it was my word over the girl who hit me. They made up one excuse after another, saying I fell asleep on the bus. They told my mom she needed to set a bedtime so I could get at least eight hours' worth of sleep.

My mom told them my bedtime was at nine. It didn't matter what was said, they would come up with another excuse to cover their butts. Why wasn't anyone concerned? In the front of my mind, all I could think about was, what about me?"

~~~

"I tried to tell my parents about what was going on at school. They would tell me I am fine because children do not have problems or worries. They would go on to say I do not have to worry about paying bills. I would tell them, that might be very well true, but I have a lot to worry about at school every single day.

My mother would say, "Well son, tell the person how they make you feel." Little does she know it is not that easy. My pops would say, "Be a man and take care of the problem. If they hit you, hit them back, if they talk about you, say something back; it's simple. What's hard about that?" I couldn't say what I wanted to say, instead, I said nothing. I said to myself, *what's the point? It's not as easy as it seems. Why bother to tell anyone? All I hear is, "Tell the teacher."* They do not do anything.

My parents tell me to come to them when I need to talk or in any trouble, but I can't help but think, do they really mean what they say? When I seek help, when I need to talk, they always blow me off with a "solution" they "think" will work. I do not have anyone to talk to. I do not have friends, my teachers do not listen, nor do my parents.

Life isn't supposed to be this difficult. Why doesn't anyone care? Children have feelings too. What about me? What about us? What about the children whose voices need to be heard? Who will be our voice when other people refuse to listen? Who?"

~~~

"Last week, my teacher yelled at me and told me to shut my mouth "right now" as she picked up my book and slammed it on the floor. She yelled at me because I yelled at a boy who punched me in the back for no reason. She yelled at me without asking me what happened. Why is it that the bad kids never get caught, but the good kids always get in trouble for no reason? I was told to go to the principal's office until class was over.

That wasn't fair to me. I tried explaining what happened but my teacher didn't want to hear what I had to say. I walked out the door, and the boy who punched me started to laugh. I looked at the teacher and she said, "Keep walking out the door. Now." I sat in the hallway for a while and then walked to the main office to call my mother.

When I spoke to my mother, she didn't believe me. She said I should have listened to the teacher. I tried explaining to my mother, I was sitting in my seat and the boy punched me in the back for no reason. My mother kept talking, saying, "I do not have time for this at work. If I do not work, I cannot provide food, clothes, shelter, and pay the bills." I said, "Yes ma'am." My parents are the type of parents who always believe the teachers are right. The teachers do not always tell the truth. Most of the time, I feel like throwing my hands in the air because in their eyes there is no truth in what I say. What about me? I matter too."

~~~

"My teacher called me stupid in front of the whole class today. My classmates started to laugh at me, and the teacher didn't say or do anything. After she called me stupid, she pulled my arm and told me to sit my butt (she said the A-word) down. I didn't know teachers were allowed to curse at students. Another student asked to use the restroom. My teacher told her she didn't have to use the restroom.

The girl had tears in her eyes, begging to use the restroom. My teacher said, "No, hold it or do it on yourself." When the girl walked out of the classroom, the teacher pulled her by her hair, and her beads fell on the floor. When the girl tried to come back into the classroom the teacher locked the door.

My teacher yelled at the remaining students in the class, saying, "This is an example of what will happen if any of you think of disrespecting me and not following my rules." I thought to myself, all of this just because a student needed to use the restroom. So, a teacher can disrespect students by calling us stupid and think nothing of it.

Who is supposed to protect the students in school? I thought the teachers were supposed to protect us. How can that be when the teachers call the students all kinds of names to their face? Ugh. I hate it here. Who cares about the students? What about me? What about us?"

~ ~ ~

Wounds and words hurt. Our children are yearning to be heard; whether it is a silent cry, crying out loud, speaking up verbally or acting out for attention: but no one is listening. However, the ones who are hurting the most are our children. We have to make time to listen. In order for things to change, we have to take action.

They are asking questions; What about me? What about us? We, as the parents, guardians, teachers, and higher authorities have to give them answers. Not invalid excuses or answers that are made of lies; we must seek answers of truth and bring them towards the light.

Our children are suffering, they want to lay down their armor. They are too tired, brittle, and weak. They do not want to fight anymore. They want to be set free of the silent killer. How can they be set free when they are sinking, drowning, full of doubt and in fear? They can't continue to be overlooked. We are their hope and we must change the course and bring them back to life. We cannot and will not give up on our children. We must put up a good fight until the battle is won and justice is served.

CHAPTER 10

Understanding the Message

CHILDREN ARE SUPPOSED TO be filled with laughter, joy, peace, and forgiveness. They shouldn't be afraid to live free and childlike. Nowadays, our children step into unknown and uncomfortable situations that make them feel helpless and hopeless.

They are falling without wings to keep them aloft. We, the parents, guardians, teachers, school administrators, and higher authorities are supposed to help our children develop their wings, as opposed to clipping them. If an eagle's wings were clipped, it wouldn't be able to soar and take over the skies.

When the silent killers – bullies, teachers, higher authorities, parents, and guardians clip our children's wings, their confidence is shattered into trillions of pieces. What it looks like in their eyes is impossible to put back together.

Our children are weighed down by hurt, worries, and pain that are inflicted on them on a daily basis. They do not think about their life's purpose, the only thoughts that run through their precious minds are survival and how to get through another day.

If we, the adults (parents, guardians, teachers, school administrators, and higher authority) do not take the time to listen to our children they will throw in the towel. They will feel lost and unworthy because they do not have anyone to represent them to bring forth justice.

Clipped wings will have caused our children to live in isolation and fear which rob our children of their birthright – which is happiness. Our children shouldn't cry silent or 'survival' tears, nor should they have to brace themselves to suit up for a battle they feel like they have to fight alone.

Now is the time to decide to make the change. It is time to take action. It is our responsibility as a parent, guardian, teacher, and higher authority to support and listen to our children. Their voices should never go unheard.

We must identify the problem. Once the problem is identified we should take action. When taking action, it shouldn't be swept up under the rug, instead, it should be taken seriously, not personally, and justice should be served by using the right protocol. Listening to our children, showing support, and most importantly, seeing results, is crucial.

From my experience, justice is never easily served. It is very frustrating to see the evidence plain, clear, front, and center. However, some teachers, higher authorities, and some parents always make up excuses to hide the truth.

From my niece's experience, the teachers who verbally, physically, and mentally bullied her took matters into their own hands. They never admitted their wrongdoing, yet they made my niece's life a living hell as she attended school every day. My niece felt like she didn't have a way out.

The higher authorities/principal didn't make it any better; they protected the teachers in their wrongdoing. When my niece reported her teacher's and principal's actions her situation became a personal matter.

In my niece's case, the teachers and higher authorities abused their power in the worst way. Their inappropriate behaviors weren't questioned. Their actions were overlooked. My niece cried for help and she was ignored. She wasn't protected, only abused and tortured. It never amazes me how some adults never take ownership of their responsibilities and the damage they cause.

Their unkind and rude behavior alone is a perfect example of why we should always give our children the benefit of the doubt. Just like my daddy said to me when I was younger, "There are always three sides of the story. Their side, your side, and the truth."

We should always reassure our children that they are never alone. Time flies by so fast that before we know it our children will be grown and living their own lives. With that being said, we should never miss a chance to empower our children. Our children's individuality is unique and we should teach them to embrace their authentic selves.

As I gathered my facts and contemplated on the problems I was having with my youngest son being bullied by the same little boy, I came to the conclusion that the teachers did all they could do on their end. Sometimes, there's only so much the teachers can do, but that doesn't mean the higher authorities/principals can't hold the student and parents responsible for their actions.

After talking to the young boy's mother, she was in denial, and she stated she was unaware of what was going on. However, after I contacted the principal it amazed me how the young boy's mother quickly changed her mind.

Sometimes the parents are the problem because they often make excuses for their children. They make the most excuses when they know their children should know better. Most of the time, those are the children who need help mentally but their parents neglect to seek help, or those are the children who run the household, and the parents let them get away with their outrageous behavior. Last but not least, sometimes, whether parents want to believe it or not, the children bully them as well. A parent/guardian has to look carefully and see if their child is acting out for attention.

Either way, the parents need to step up to the plate to discipline their children. They need to do their part and join in their children's lives to dissect what is going on, and what they can do to help.

Our children shouldn't have to think something is wrong with them because the parents/guardians, teachers or higher authorities feel as though our children's voices are invalid.

Our children shouldn't have to wonder, "What about us?" because some parents/guardians, teachers, school administrators, and higher authorities neglected to step out, to dare to be different and make the right choice by not tolerating bullying.

I firmly believe that we can prevent the silent killer from permanently damaging our children. The first step is for the teacher to report it to the parents and higher authorities, or vice versa. Secondly, the higher authorities should discipline the bully so that other students and parents will see that bullying isn't allowed. Thirdly, the parents/guardians should stop being in denial and discipline their children as well.

If the bullying behavior doesn't improve, the parents should seek help for their child. If the parents neglect to seek help or if there isn't anything wrong with the child, after they seek help, and the bullying continues, then the parents/guardians should be held responsible for their child's behavior.

If a teacher is a bully, they should be fired because a teacher doesn't have the right to "restrain" a child by choking, throwing books, angrily yelling, and being out of control in general. That is unacceptable. It should be recognized and dealt with as soon as possible without any excuses – and no exceptions.

We have to look beneath the surface and work our way up to the core to ask hard questions; to put a fire under those who are accountable for mistreating our children. We cannot surrender to their senseless excuses.

We have to dig for resources that will work in our favor. It will not be an easy task but we must be persistent to work towards seeing results. When it comes to bullying, there is no such thing as negotiating. We must hit the ground running and trust our vision because our children are our priorities. Therefore, we must keep striving, fighting, and pushing until we change the course of justice for our children.

As we work on change for the better, we should go above and beyond to help deepen our relationships with our children. We have to help our children to embrace, accept, and express themselves as they are.

Building a relationship, foundation, and confidence in our children is how they learn to love themselves, accept their flaws, and dance to the beat of their own drum. After all, they are a reflection of us – we are our children's foundation.

When paving the foundation for our children at a young age we have to instill in their minds not to worry about what other's think or say about them because we cannot please and make everyone happy. We have to remind them constantly not to connect their self-worth to other people's words and thoughts, for their actions, are a personal matter they have with themselves.

We have to teach our children that they have a voice, and they can roar as loud as they want. We have to instill in our children not to deny their abilities in making a difference by speaking up and coming to us for help. Most importantly, we have to let our children know there is no such thing as being held down by someone else's opinions of them. Other's thoughts are like confetti. They don't matter, and they fade away just like smoke from a fire.

As they grow, they will start to pave another layer of their foundation as we step aside, but not too far. Although it will seem as though they do not need our help, from time to time we need to step in to let them know life is about both disappointment and achievements.

Life is a force to be reckoned with but it creates perseverance and helps them to determine a life that is rightly theirs. We have to let them know the script changes for the better, and at times for the worse, therefore, boundaries are important, but life is never a limitation of hope or possibilities.

We have to keep in mind when our children are young and depend on us, we are our children's hope, great strength, motivator, protector, and so much more. At that point in time, it is critical, because it can make or break their confidence, self-esteem, strength, fears, happiness, and sadness.

We do not want our children to start off at an early age where their confidence is shot down because we didn't listen. We don't want them to underestimate themselves by thinking less of themselves because their self-esteem has accumulated so much doubt from their early days.

We do not want them to think the only way to gain strength is to be hurt, in pain, and alone. We do not want them to live in fear because they think there is no such thing as hope. We do not want them to think happiness comes just by pleasing others and neglecting themselves.

We do not want them to tip the scale and think sadness is a one-way street that leads to suicide, by only thinking negative thoughts and not having a purpose to live.

The foundation of youth starts with us as the parents, guardians, teachers, school administrators, higher authorities, and so many more people in the community. It will build inner strength within our children if they see that we care by our actions – listening and being there for them when the battle is too hard for them to fight alone.

We have to be their voice because when they are young, we are molding them to become great people. Once they see their voices matter and deserve to be heard, that develops confidence, balance, personal growth, and self-love within themselves.

When my sons told me about them being bullied, I immediately took charge. I asked them if they spoke with their teachers. They assured me they did on several occasions. However, they weren't happy with the results. I went in full force in a respectful way, to get down to solving the problem.

When my daughter knew she was being mistreated on several occasions, I stepped up to the plate because I wasn't going to let what she encountered be ignored.

Once a parent lets their children's problems sink in the sand, they will not have confidence in us and will seek help elsewhere; and who knows where?

I believe for every problem there is a solution. It is a matter of how far we are willing to go. Sacrificing time will have its highs and lows, up and downs. It will be difficult, but we will be reclaiming our children's entitlement to a happy life.

It will be well worth it. We will gain energy from creating what the higher authorities thought was nothing and not important, and turning it into something, especially when they feel our point of view is irrelevant. They will fuel our fire with nonsense, excuses, and lies – which is exactly what we need to fight the battle our children are fighting every single day. Therefore, we must not hesitate to obtain justice for our children.

I am the type of person who, if I know there's something that can be done, I will get it done, regardless of how hard it gets or what I have to go through. I know the harder I work, the better the results will be in my favor.

When it comes to my children, if they feel that they are being treated unfairly and they are unhappy, then that's a problem. Believe me, there are no ifs, ands, or butts about it – I do not want to hear any excuses – I want and will see results!

When my children see how hard I will fight for them, it builds their confidence, and they know without a doubt Momma is going to solve the problem. After they see the problem has been taken care of, they are so happy and appreciate me making their lives and their days a lot better. They are able to breathe, let go, and release. A child's concern shouldn't go unnoticed, it should be brought into the light and nipped in the bud the first time around.

We shouldn't ever be too busy nor should we procrastinate when our children are asking for our help, or if their actions are speaking louder than their words.

Our children's confidence should be sky-high, and they should travel effortlessly without the silent killer putting negative thoughts and fear in their minds. They should know their parents are winds of change because we gather their needs and turn them into strength, courage, and wisdom as they develop patiently while the transformation is taking place.

Our children should have courage and be able to fly fearlessly with keen eyesight because they know without a doubt their parents and guardians will take care of what is too much for them to bear. They have an advantage – we are their caretakers; therefore, they should spread their wings, take flight, and reach above the clouds where dreams do come true.

Our children have a purpose in life, and what beautiful lives they have ahead of them, filled with prosperity and abundance.

They shouldn't smile through the pain or fuel their sadness, because the silent killer is stealing their joy. Instead, they should have freedom—that is filled with peace and balance in their lives.

We should take time to think and analyze. As parents and guardians, we shouldn't take any shortcuts. We have to look at our children's situation from every angle.

When the challenge is hard because the higher authorities are ignoring us too, we should never give up. Our load might become heavy but our children are a part of us; they are a reflection of us; and we want our children to know and feel they are safe, loved, and wanted.

The higher authorities always speak of change, changing for the better, yet most of the time they do not practice what they preach. We all can make room for change; we all can make room for improvement because one shouldn't have to handle anything alone.

When all hope is gone, we have to let our children know why they are here, and why they are alive. We have to reassure them that lies can't live forever. We have to show them that their voices are powerful and they should never be afraid to speak up and speak their truth.

One thing's for sure, as parents and guardians we have to be cautious about what we hear and see. When fighting for our children we have to keep in mind that other people will try their hardest to make us give in. They are going to treat our children unfairly in the process. They will become uncaring, and try to shut us down mentally, physically, and emotionally. Furthermore, they will try to block us and shut every door to hide the truth. Little do they know, regardless of what they have in mind, justice will prevail because we are not giving up!

They will pull out every tactic there is to use. However, we must put up a good fight. We must refuse to shut down. They can try to take it all, but one thing they cannot take from us is our voice. They will try to silence our children and keep them in darkness. What they fail to realize is that our children are a part of us, and when we all come together as one, we will have a mighty roar that will be unstoppable and finally heard.

CHAPTER 11

Atlanta Neighborhood Charter School (ANCS) Journey

WE WANT TO PROTECT our children by any means necessary. Sadly, we cannot be with them every moment of the day. I never thought I would have to teach my children to defend themselves at such a young age. Children are supposed to be filled with free-spirits and dreams of limitless opportunities. They are supposed to be filled with light that shines with happiness and joy, that shouldn't be dim or filled with darkness and fear.

Children should be living a carefree life and always smiling, laughing filled with peace, and harmony; not worrying about the troubles of what tomorrow will bring. Our children should have a wide range of imagination and think about the greatest mysteries that they think of accomplishing; not making sacrifices of giving up their clothes, lunch money, or being robbed of their personality, and striped from their self-esteem.

As parents, guardians, teachers, and higher authorities we are our children's *better days*, we are the outcome of their future, we are the pieces of the puzzle that could put their shattered confidence back together. When our children are hopeless we are the light that shines brightly to renew their hope. Our love and actions are hope that floats to restore what was lost and to renew strength that they never imagine existed.

We are our children's voices when all else has failed. As parents, guardians, and teachers we have to be more involved in our children's lives.

Bullying shouldn't be taken lightly. Sadly, bullying is played down in school, some teachers, administrators, and sometimes at home by the parents.

We have to change this continuous cycle. It has gone on too far for way too long. Our children shouldn't be victims of suicide or have suicidal thoughts, because someone think they have the ability to strip them bit by bit and piece by piece of their birthright of life.

We must fight for our children; our voices are louder and the roar of our forthcoming for change will be heard loud and clear. We will burn the ashes of fear from our children because we are a source of empowerment.

Our children are someone special, they are someone unique, they are a gift, and they are our children that we love dearly. Without a doubt, change will come and we must make that change happen because bullying is not accept.

We shouldn't give anyone the ability to rob our children from happiness. We have the power to change the situation. For those who feel as though bullying is an unknown situation, let's dare to be different and make the situation known by opening the problem at hand—by speaking up and finding a solution to the problem. We should always remember when a problem occurs, we must not forget, there's always a solution to solve the problem.

Now is the time to decide to make the change. Now is the time to dissect and look at every angle in the distasteful world of bullying. Now is the time for us to put our best foot forward and take on the responsibility of saving our children from being killed or destroyed from bullying also known as the Silent Killer. Our children shouldn't be a prisoner from what a bully has cast on them.

The time has come to take action to stop bullying and the time is now.

My children and I have a long history with Atlanta Neighborhood Charter School (ANCS). My eldest son, who is 21 years old, attended ANCS from 2nd through 8th grade. My daughter, who is 17 years old, attended ANCS from K through 8th grade.

When my oldest son attended the elementary school campus at that time it was called Neighborhood Charter School (NCS). During that era, NCS had a higher percentage of minorities than it has in 2019. I might add that minorities were accepted and treated fairly by the principal and some faculty and staff. The principal followed the guidelines, rules, and regulations, and she made everyone feel welcome. Most importantly, I don't recall having any issues with bullying at NCS when she was in the leadership position. When the principal departed from NCS, I was devastated because I knew from that point on NCS was never going to be the same.

After the principal left, another took her place. However, she stayed for a short period of time at NCS. Most importantly, I must say if my oldest son had an issue with another student, which was very rare, the principal who replaced the best leadership at NCS handled the issue, nipped it in the bud, and my son and I never had the same problem recur twice.

After the other principal took over, our current principal then became the assistant principal. Which I strongly disagreed with. At that time, when our present principal received the promotion to be the assistant principal, she was the Curriculum and Assessment Specialist. Prior to that, she taught 5th grade at ANCS and 6th, 4th and 2nd grade for another county. Although our present principal might have an educational background, in my opinion, she did not and does not have the proper training or hands-on experience to handle a full load of responsibilities.

When the recent principal departed from her short term as the principal at NCS, the assistant principal (who is the current principal now at ANCS—2019) was promoted to the position of principal. That was one of the biggest mistakes NCS made. The issue with ANCS as it stands today is—they promote through "in house." I feel that our current principal (2019) did and still does not have enough experience under her belt. The reason being that she wasn't the assistant principal long enough to take on hundreds of students and double-digit numbers of faculty and staff. ANCS board should have hired someone more qualified to take over when the previous principal left.

When our current principal became principal, ANCS went downhill. She doesn't know how to communicate with others. The rules were made up as she, the principal, decided. Sadly, ANCS board promoted another teacher (who is no longer assistant principal at ANCS elementary campus) to be the assistant principal, who also didn't have enough experience for the job. Prior to being assistant principal, she taught kindergarten through 2nd grade in Fulton County and her role at ANCS was being the math instructor for special needs. I might add, she was hired from "in house" as well.

My youngest son recently graduated from ANCS (elementary campus) in 2019. When he was in kindergarten, our current principal was the principal and the assistant principal (who is no longer assistant principal at ANCS elementary campus) did not and still until this day does not know how to control and take bullying seriously. Bullying now, as it was then, is at an all-time high, and is covered up by one excuse after another.

When my youngest son was in kindergarten, his teachers tried their best to confront bullying, however, it was never-ending. I must say, my son was passive because he didn't know what "bullying" was—needless to say, he was a baby (6 years old).

When my son was promoted to 1st grade, bullying was bad at ANCS. This is when I experienced a rude awakening and a clear understanding that a high percentage of the teachers, faculty, staff, and higher authorities did not know how to control the bullying that was traumatizing the students. After bullying repeatedly occurred at ANCS when my son was in 1st grade, I had a parent-teacher conference, which was not successful. A couple of months later, I had a parent, student, teacher, and assistant principal conference, and that most definitely was distasteful. As my son and I sat face-to-face in the colorfully decorated classroom, words were being placed in my son's mouth. We were told that he was basically making up the bullying issues that had occurred. I was taken aback when a teacher who taught at ANCS took her son out of the school because her son too was being bullied by the same boy. I had to gather my thoughts and I asked everyone who was in the meeting, "Are you all saying my son is making up being bullied?" They asked my son if he knew the difference between being bullied and when someone had done something by "mistake."

One day, when I picked my son up from school, he was holding his tummy, telling me he was in pain. I asked him what was wrong; he told me that as he was going to art class and as he bent to tie his shoe, the entire class kicked him. The art teacher (who taught at ANCS since my oldest attended), stated she wasn't aware of this. The principal and the assistant principal called a student and asked her where my son was sitting in art class. They believed a 1st grader over my son. What the principal should have done was ask the art teacher what happened and why didn't she address the issue. I took him to the emergency room to have him checked out and to have documents for my records. It was an uphill battle trying to have my son's 1st-grade teachers, principal, and assistant principal understand my son's state of depression. Needless to say, excuses were given and nothing was done.

During 2nd-grade, my son's teachers did not tolerate bullying in their class. However, the bullying took place during recess, lunch, and as my son waited for his number to be called during the car rider line. I sent his teachers, the principal, assistant principal (at the present time), and the special education teachers an email and asked if we all could have a meeting. I was very emotional in the meeting because I have a diverse family and felt as though my son was being mistreated because of his color. I wasn't the only parent of color at ANCS who felt this way (I noticed there were fewer children of color at ANCS because minority parents made the decision to withdraw their children from the school because they were treated unfairly). I asked the principal and assistant principal (at the time) if they did not like black people because when we had an issue at ANCS it seemed as if our issues were continuously being ignored. I must say, the meeting was not successful.

The principal shed a tear, however, I explained to her, she shed a tear, but my son has shed many tears over the course of the years at ANCS. I must say, one of my son's teachers who was disturbed by the meeting decided to resign from his/her position less than a week from when the meeting took place. That alone spoke volumes. During the end of his 2nd-grade year, a teacher from ANCS called me and made me aware that my son was being bullied that particular day, however, that time around my son took up for himself. The teacher called me and said, "I want to let you know, I saw exactly what happened. I'm calling you, just in case someone tells you something different. Please tell your son, I am so proud of him for finally taking up for himself."

Third grade was the worst year ever. I felt as though my son's teachers did not know how to handle bullying. I had so many parents, teachers, and student conferences one after another (face-to-face and phone conferences). However, I was told my son made up assumptions about him being bullied. There was one excuse after another as the principal, assistant principal, and I had a parent-teacher conference over the phone. I was told that the bully had an issue. However, to my understanding, my son's bully clearly understood what he was doing. He understood the words, "No", "Stop", and "Leave me alone." Yet the bully purposely continued to bully my son. The principal and assistant principal didn't make the situation any better, because all I heard were endless, unacceptable, and senseless excuses one after another—as if they were trying to cover up and take up for the bully. Which didn't make any sense to me.

My son tried to commit suicide. I was devastated because my son tried to take his life because ANCS let his issues go unnoticed. I lost a lot of sleep and I had to seek help for my son because I was afraid I was going to lose him. I called the bully's mother, and she stated that she didn't have a clue about it. I talked to the principal and told her I thought she made the child's mother aware of what was going on. She stated, "As you say you spoke to her...." (As if I was lying). I made it clear I did speak with her, and she was unaware of what was going on. Long story short, the parent admitted she knew what was going on but she didn't know the entire story. I was very frustrated because what my son was going through was a joke to them.

In 4th grade, my son had the best teachers ever! Fourth grade was the first, last, and the only peaceful year we had at ANCS (Elementary Campus). I knew right then and there, the problem was the parents, his previous teachers, the principal, and assistant principal who didn't know how to control bullying and/or didn't take bullying seriously enough to want to control the deadly issue. I loved his 4th-grade teachers and appreciate them until this day.

5th grade (end of the year 2019), was beyond miserable. It seemed like every single day there was a problem. I shouldn't have been surprised because he had the same teachers as he had during 3rd-grade. The issue that I have with ANCS (Elementary campus) is that they do not understand how and when the bullying starts.

During K-3rd grades, my son was passive. People would verbally, mentally, emotionally, and physically abuse him, yet nothing was ever done. The reason for this was because my son made their job easy because he didn't fight back. They brushed everything under the rug because it wasn't an important matter to them—because it would have taken up too much of their time. During K-3rd all I heard was—my son needed to tell the teachers. He did, but nothing was done. Another thing I do not understand about the ANCS elementary campus – they appear to have the mindset that "apologizing" solves problems. They feel as though when one student apologizes to another that it's the end of the issue. No, it is not the end of the problem, because the problem was never solved. The problem was never taken seriously by an adult.

ANCS always says, "Tell a teacher." However, when the student tells the teacher, the teacher ignores the student, or asks the other student to apologize—then they think everything is okay—end of the story—end of the problem. No, the problem has accumulated because the bully knows he/she will only have to apologize and do the exact same thing again, or worse.

ANCS has formed a habit of saying, "Kids will be kids." No, kids will not be kids in this day and age—children are so mean, cruel, and so disrespectful. At ANCS the disrespectful students and their parents run the school – they get away with everything. It seems like they are the ones who call the shots. It's either their way or no way—and the board, teachers, principals, assistant principal, and higher authorities are afraid to speak up. Not only are they afraid to speak up, but they are also afraid to give the students who are disrespectful, the students who bully other students, the consequences they deserve. Instead, they get a gentle slap on the wrist, a little talking-to (referral), a hug, and sent back to class.

When my son started taking up for himself in 5th grade (after five years of being tortured), that became a serious problem at ANCS. It seemed like three times or more every month my son was in the principal's office. A young boy took and hid my son's bookbag (during dismissal); however, nothing was done, the teacher said to the young boy, "Give him his bookbag back." The boy wouldn't give it back. Yet he laughed at my son and kept saying over and over, "I know where your bookbag is at." My son had had enough, and took the boy's bookbag and threw it down the stairs. The boy cried and everyone ran to his rescue — and my son was punished all because someone touched my son's belongings first.

A couple of weeks later, in art class, two boys took my son's pencil and threw it across the room. As always, the art teacher didn't see or notice anything. My son asked them to get his pencil, both boys said no. They took turns and made fun of my son's artwork. The boys kept bullying my son as they got pencil scraps from the pencil sharpener and poured them over my son's head. Again, the art teacher didn't see anything (so she says). The young boys took it up a notch and threw erasers at my son's chest (my son has asthma). My son said that is enough, as he picked one of the boys up and slammed him on the floor. The art teacher ran to the boy's rescue and said to my son, "Oh my gosh, you are going to hurt him!" My son was sent to the assistant principal's office (The current assistant principal now—2019. I might add, she was promoted from "in—house" as well), who isn't qualified to be an assistant principal. She only has experience working at a couple of elementary school campuses, which is not enough experience to be responsible for an entire school. She, just like most of the teachers and staff at ANCS was focused only on how it ended. She didn't care about how it started. She pressured my son to give the two boys an apology. My son sat in her office for the rest of the day and missed out on recess and his classes. The other boys went to recess and to their classes. I spoke with the assistant principal, she said, "Putting hands on another student is not allowed at

ANCS." I told her, torturing a student should not be tolerated either. Those boys provoked my son to put his hands on them. Sad, to say, the assistant principal didn't see where I was coming from. She skipped over how it started.

A couple of weeks later, my son was working on his assignment until a student decided he wanted to invade my son's space, and he took it upon himself to cut off my son's iPad. My son cut his iPad back on and asked the boy to stop. This went back and forth five times until my son threw the boy's book. The boy continued to invade my son's space until he got a reaction from my son—my son pushed him. Guess who got in trouble? My son. He was told to go to the principal's office. Again, I met with the assistant principal and one of my son's 5th-grade teachers. His teacher's excuse was—she was the only teacher in the classroom, therefore she didn't see anything. What sense did that make? Being the only teacher in class, she should have had her eyes wide open. Most definitely, she should have heard my son ask the boy to stop cutting his iPad off numerous times. She should have seen and heard a book being thrown. The question is—what was she doing?

My son got in trouble. He sat in the assistant principal's office all day. However, his teacher and assistant principal neglected to acknowledge how it started. The assistant principal held my son in her office because he wouldn't apologize (as he shouldn't), and she asked my son to make a commitment to not put hands on another student. I expressed my thoughts and said, "You're basically telling my son to put his life on the line, get his butt beat, not to defend himself, and die." The assistant principal asked my son why he was so angry. His teacher sat in the chair as if she didn't have a clue. I wasn't going to let my son scramble for the answer, because he looked overwhelmed from being interrogated all day. I said, "Because he is tired!" I looked at his teacher and said, "You know my son's history, you know he's been bullied for years. We've only had one year of peace." His teacher said, "But he shouldn't put hands on anyone." I said, "In the state of Georgia, bullying is when someone invades someone's space on purpose and when someone purposely interferes with someone's learning. This is what's happening here." I added, "If these children didn't touch my son or his things over and over again after he asked them to please stop, they wouldn't have gotten hit. What is it that you do not understand? It always starts somewhere."

Three weeks before the end of school, my son was written up and had In-School Suspension (ISS), because a young boy kept stepping on the heel of his shoe. My son turned around and asked the young boy to please stop. The boy laughed and continued to step on my son's heel. My son told one of his teachers. He said, "He keeps hitting the heel of my shoe." His teacher brushed it off and said, "No, that is not called hitting." Since the teacher didn't do anything about it, the boy continued. My son again asked him to stop, but the boy said, "Stop what? This?" as he kept saying, "Oops, oops, oops, oops, oops" He stepped on my son's heel each time he said, "Oops." (which was 5 times). My son then defended himself and punched the boy in the stomach. Needless to say, everyone ran to the boy's rescue.

My son's teacher and the assistant principal talked to both boys. The boy admitted he did it on purpose. However, my son still got in trouble. The assistant principal wrote on the referral that my son would have ISS because he put hands on someone. I was very upset as I told her, "You all here at ANCS have the wool pulled over your eyes because you do not care how these incidents start." I slammed the paper on her desk and told her I was not signing anything and I walked out of the office. What made matters worse, the boy admitted that he repeatedly stepped on my son's heel on purpose. To add insult to injury, the assistant principal wrote on my son's referral sheet for ISS that my son said, 'Please, stop stepping on the back of my heel', and that the boy admitted he stepped on my son's heel repeatedly on purpose. Yet, my son was to blame.

On our way home, my son expressed to me how the assistant principal and the principal, were always rude to him when I wasn't around. More so slick-talking and being disrespectful. My son said to both the assistant principal and principal that he didn't deserve to be punished. They told my son, "Well if you kept your hands to yourself you wouldn't be in trouble." Honestly, I was upset, because how "mature" of them to blame a child for defending himself. If they handled the bullying as it occurred/started, then a child wouldn't have to put hands on anyone. Instead of my son sitting in the assistant principal's office all day Friday, I kept him home. I kept him home because for once I wanted to have one day of peace. Just one day.

After the Milestone testing was over, I picked my son up from school early because he had a doctor's appointment. I was told by the receptionist he was outside at recess. I walked to the recess field and I was told by one teacher he was getting some water. The art teacher, joyfully said, "Oh no, he is in the assistant principal's office." My heart began to race as I ran off the field into the building, wondering what had happened now. After running up the steps, I quickly walked down the hall, knocked on the assistant principal's door. To my surprise, my son was sitting in a chair looking helpless as he was being double-teamed by both the principal and assistant principal.

The principal was shocked as she tried to cover it up with a smile and said, "Hi!" The assistant principal looked as if she was in control of the situation as she was leaning against the table. I asked them, "What is the problem now?" They said, "Nothing, we want your son to apologize to the boy for hitting him in the stomach." I told them, "He is not going to apologize. He stayed home for what someone did to him. He will not apologize." I was breathing hard because I was/am so tired of this. I was very upset as I told them we were not doing this today. I told my son to go get his bookbag so we could leave. I felt like they were interrogating my son, and what made matters worse, they were interrogating him without my knowledge.

They called me when my son "supposedly" did something to someone else, yet he got in trouble for it. However, they didn't call me to be in the "meeting" as they pulled my son out of class to pressure him and try to make him apologize for what someone did to him first. What sense does that make? The principal said, "That student was injured." I looked at her and said, "If he would have kept his foot on the floor as my son repeatedly asked him nicely to stop, and when my son told the teacher she completely ignored him, and the student repeatedly did it on purpose as he admitted it.

110

If he would have kept his foot on the floor and stopped when my son asked him to, then he wouldn't have been injured." I told her my son was injured badly when he was kicked by the entire class. The principal turned around, looked at me, and said, "So you keep saying that happened." As if she didn't remember, she didn't care then and doesn't care now. (That wasn't the first time the principal made a, "So you keep saying that happened." smart comment. When my son was bullied in 3rd grade, I called the bully's parents. I talked to the principal and made her aware. She said, "So you say, you talked to the student's parents." Indeed, for a fact I did. Another time, I sent the principal an email expressing my concerns when she and the current assistant principal spoke with my son without my knowing. **Quoting the principal, "Good morning, thank you for recounting the events of this past year from your perspective."** The principal speaks/communicates as if she doesn't care and turns a blind eye to what is happening in front of her at ANCS).

I looked at her and said, "It did happen, I have proof from the hospital." I left the office and left the building with my son.

As I took him to the doctor's office. I made the doctor and nurse aware of the situation, that way they will have it for their records.

What bothered me, if the little boy was injured so badly, why corner my son (a child) and pressure him for an apology. Why not call me—the parent? What is the purpose of a principal and assistant principal bullying a child for an apology for which he paid the unfair consequences because of what someone had done to him? How is that fair? If this was an important matter—why wasn't I (the parent) aware they were going pull my son from recess (again) for something that happened a week ago—my son honored his unfair punishment. I'm still trying to understand why the principal and assistant principal were being so secretive.

As I was explaining to my son's physician and nurse, what doesn't add up is—my children are always respectful. We have rules and regulations in our household. My children respect others and expect the same in return (which is extremely rare). My children never ever started a fight, invaded other people's space, disturbed someone or interrupted class. From kindergarten through 4thgrade my son received a satisfactory in conduct. His teachers always say my son is so well mannered, listens, pays attention, and is such a sweetheart. I know, because I raised my children that way. However, his year in 5th grade he had an unsatisfactory conduct because he stood his ground. Never has my son had a referral because he put hands on someone first, it was always because of what someone did to him. How is that fair? How can parents, teachers, and higher authorities of the school (assistant principals and principals) turn a blind eye—it is because they do not care.

The last week of school, I received a phone called from my son's teacher. She expressed to me that my son called a student "fat." Although I wasn't present—I voiced my assumption of what I thought may have happened. The reason for this—the same day before my son prepared himself for school, he asked me could he stay home. I asked him why. He said because every day it is an issue with the line. People always jump me in line, call me names, and nothing is ever done. He went on to say, a girl jumped him in line the day before, called him ugly told him his clothes and shoes were ugly and got in his face. My son has told me many stories like this one. I told him, "Well if you do not mind, try your best to ignore the name-calling. How about you just get in the back of the line. That way, nobody will jump you in line, and you will have your own space." My son felt like that wasn't fair. Indeed, it wasn't. However, I told him, "We only have two more days in school, we are not giving in, we are being the bigger person, and we want peace."

Well… I was correct about why the teacher was calling. The teacher said, yes, the girl called my son names, but it didn't give him the right to call her fat, because calling her fat hurt the girl's feeling. The teacher went on to say, "I am sick of the student (she was talking about my son), acting like the victim." Wow, I was taken aback. She said, "Because he gets away with a lot." I begged to differ. I was like—here we go again. I asked her, "You really think my son gets away with a lot, after someone put hands on him first, touches his things first, starts things with him first, and he gets in trouble for things he didn't do is your definition that he gets away with a lot?" I told her, "We will be on the phone all day because I am not going to tell you all what you all want to hear." I added," The girl shouldn't have called my son names—then she wouldn't have been called a name as well." Long story short—my son had to sit outside the classroom while his teacher spoke to me over the phone (the girl was in class, learning). Which wasn't fair, because she jumped my son in line, called him names (which the teacher knew, yet, once again, my son was in trouble for defending himself, and this time around for what someone said to him).

When my son was sitting outside the classroom, the art teacher walked by and asked my son why he was sitting outside the classroom. My son told her because he called someone fat. The art teacher didn't know the entire story, however, she sarcastically said to my son, "Oh, that is called bullying." As a parent, I was upset because she was mocking me as a parent because for years I've been complaining to ANCS about bullying. I knew she was mocking me and my son. Her remark was very immature and distasteful.

One could ask, why didn't I transfer my son out of the school? I had my reasons—first, my son has a speech disability and he was progressing with the speech teacher he'd had since 1st grade. If I moved him, he would have to adjust to someone new, and maybe fall behind.

Second, ANCS' academic rating, in my eyes, is fair, I liked how my son engaged with his lessons. I love, love, love his speech therapy teachers, and I must say ANCS Special Education Department really cares for their students. They always put their best foot forward and work hard for what is best for my son's education.

Third, as a parent, bullying is an issue statewide, and if I moved him to another school, there was a possibility that the issue would occur again.

Fourth, ANCS is known for making issues difficult and extremely hard for minorities. At times, I felt like they purposely treated minorities unfairly so that minority parents would voluntarily transfer their students out of the school. We, as parents, shouldn't have to move our children here and there because other parents and the school system lack the ability to handle bullying, and to treat everyone with respect and dignity, regardless of race, gender, religion, etc.

ANCS elementary school needs to realize they are the reason why our children think of committing suicide because they help the bullies by making up senseless excuses, as opposed to caring for the children who are being bullied. ANCS Elementary (the principal, assistant principal, and some teachers) will leave your child filled with doubt. They will make your child think he/she is wrong as they tend to put words and thoughts into the student's head. ANCS elementary will try to manipulate your children to think it is all their fault. They have certain students who they favor, and most of those students are bullies. I think ANCS is afraid of losing funds from parents who are wealthy. They are very good at making your child think he/she is in the wrong as they twist their words, and make them feel as though they are making up what happened to them.

I had an issue at ANCS middle school campus when my daughter was in 7th grade. A young boy was leaning on the wall as my daughter was walking down the hall, talking to her friends with her books in her hand, and the young boy purposely tripped my daughter. Little did he know he was going to feel the pain as my daughter defended herself and kicked him in his private area. Like always, when a student is in the wrong, everyone runs to his/her rescue. I was told my daughter had one day of suspension and two days of ISS (In-School Suspension) and the boy didn't have any consequence.

I spoke to the current middle school principal as she was sorting out the letters to put on the announcement board—she didn't make eye contact (which was very unprofessional, rude, and disrespectful on so many levels—as if what I was saying wasn't important. I must say that, from my experience, the current principal at the middle school campus is always rude, she has a smart, and sarcastic response to everything. For the parents' and students' sake, I hope she has improved her attitude over the years) as she said (with an 'I do not care, nasty, and carefree attitude') "I don't know what happened." I asked her, "How can you call yourself a leader if you don't know what is going on in your school?" She asked me to talk to the assistant principal. I did, but little did she know the conversation wasn't over. I emailed her how I felt. I am more than sure she didn't want to read the truth. Later that evening, she called me. We talked and I touched base with her about my thoughts and her sarcastic remarks—as I let her know I am not the one who takes sarcastic remarks to heart because I am not a child. I am an adult and all about business, therefore, her smart mouth is not welcome.

As we addressed the issue for about an hour, she humbly apologized. I felt as though she and I had an understanding.

The current middle school assistant principal is an amazing assistant principal, he is always willing to listen and solve the issue at hand. We as parents want someone to LISTEN, COMMUNICATE, and UNDERSTAND. As parents, after we talk about the issue—we need to see action/results—and that is what the middle school assistant principal does. When I had an issue with my daughter and her teacher, he sat in the meeting as a mediator, gave his honest advice, and I never had any issues with that teacher after the conference. I truly appreciate him for that. We need more leaders like him to be the foundation of our schools.

Sadly, ANCS elementary school campus covers up bullying and they never admit to their mistakes. The problem is that the students control the school. The parents who have a student who is a bully, never punish their child—and that is one reason why bullying isn't taken seriously. Learning starts at home (I am a firm believer in that), however, if "home" cannot take care of the issue, the school needs to raise the bar, and hold the bully accountable for what they have done, regardless of how the parent feels, and regardless of how much money the parents donate to the school. Everyone needs to be treated equally.

ANCS Elementary School is known for breaking the state of Georgia Bullying Laws:

ANCS says hitting isn't allowed. First and foremost, bullying shouldn't be allowed. Invading someone's space shouldn't be allowed. Damaging someone's belongings shouldn't be allowed. When someone says stop, it should be taken seriously and not brushed to the side and ignored. They shouldn't wait until the situation escalates then make an irrational decision when the end results have taken a turn for the worse (a student putting hands on someone as he/she defends themselves from being tortured over and over again after constantly saying no/stop and/or being abused by another person).

I think ANCS needs to stop putting inexperienced staff and faculty from "in house" in charge of others. They need to put people who have hands-on experience as well as those with the educational background to care and take our children's words, emotions, thoughts, and what they are going through seriously. Our children's voices matter. They should be taken seriously. Nowadays, children are under so much stress and peer pressure—they need someone to listen and take their issues seriously. Example: A major cooperation would not promote someone from a lower level or without experience to be CEO. ANCS shouldn't do that either.

Over the years, I've experienced a handful of minorities as lead teachers at ANCS (if it was that many). As ANCS focus on preventing bullying, they also need to take into consideration the option to hire more minorities as faculty and staff. As a bonus, ANCS needs to hire more minorities as lead teachers as well.

Atlanta Public Schools do not take bullying seriously either. I reached out to the House of Representatives and state Senators as well. I might add, I am pleased to say, some responded to my concerns. Sadly, Atlanta Public School Student Discipline Coordinator reached out to me after I voiced my concerns. She asked me if I could have a meeting once again with the Principal at ANCS, to whom I've voiced my deepest concerns since kindergarten regarding my son. The Student Discipline Coordinator's "brilliant idea" quote: "Would you be willing to attend a meeting at the school this Monday after 12 p.m.? If so, please respond to this email so that I can let the school know and I can plan to attend also. I think it will be great if we can all put our heads together to hear your concerns and brainstorm ways that we can ensure that Elijah will be both successful and safe for the last week of school."

I was highly disappointed and declined the invite. They wanted to "put our heads together to hear my concerns and brainstorm on ways that we can ensure my son will have both a successful and safe LAST WEEK of school."

As if she hadn't read the same emails and documents I attached concerning the issues I was having at ANCS. My voice and concerns went over their heads.

I am so tired of people making excuses for bullying. I am so tired of the school system trying to ease their conscience by acting as though they care. They feel like, if they meet up with you, hear you out, then the damage is fixed. They feel like, oh, the issue is solved—as they wash their hands and move on with their lives. No, it is not solved or fixed. The right thing to do will be to hear the parent's concerns, take it seriously, do something about it, put actions to their words and "concerns" they are supposed to have. Sadly, their actions and words are counterfeit because they act as though they are concerned, but in reality, they show their true colors when they sleep on the problem. I was at an all-time loss when I was thinking to myself *what happened to wanting my son to have a successful and safe last 6 years of elementary school (K-5)?* I am tired of talking and having a "meeting." After talking for years and years, something needs to be done and actions need to be taken.

My response to the email:

"Student Discipline Coordinator,
 I left you a voicemail as well.
 However, I will have to decline the offer. I've spoken with the principal for years and years and years, yet nothing has changed for the better.
 I'm tired of talking. Actions need to be taken.
 I'm taking my son out of APS schools altogether. I've made the decision to homeschool him since reports of bullying ALWAYS end up falling on deaf ears.
 I will continue to work hard and push for a bill to be passed holding everyone accountable for their actions.
 It's time out for talking and singing the same song over and over again. It's time out for making excuses one after another. It's

time out for covering up the deadliest issue in the world, something has to change—and I'm going to be that change.

I'm tired. My son is tired. We are tired.

Our children's voices deserve to be heard. They deserve to live a prosperous and abundant life. They deserve to know someone, at least one person, cares. Our children's lives matter!

Thank you kindly.

Have a blessed weekend as well."

I might add that I sent APS Superintended an email, however, I never received a response. I reached out to the Georgia Charter Schools Association but sadly, I didn't receive a response from them either. I reached out to ANCS Executive Director. He made time to listen and talk about my issues, which I appreciate. However, I am wondering, is his mindset the same as the other administrators? Did he meet up with me just to say, well I listened to her, now the issue is solved. Or is he really going to take what I said, and other parent's concerns, into consideration and help be the change for the better for our children? At this moment in time, I have no hope in the school system, my mindset is that I will believe it when I see change.

I contacted other people as well, it never amazes me how we as a community, as "the people" vote for the representatives in office, but most of them say they cannot help. 90% of the time I heard, "I am so sorry to hear what your son is going through, although, I cannot help, here is someone who can." Every time someone referred me to someone else—sadly, they said the same thing, "I am so sorry for what your son is going through, however, I cannot help, but here is a contact name and number who will be able to help." .... Needless to say, the same song was played over and over again. Another issue begins to come to mind as I ask myself, *why do I vote?* I asked myself countless times, *why do I vote if everyone says, we are sorry for what you and your son are going through, but ridiculously they cannot help or they are not willing to help.*

Out of 356 emails I sent to House of Representatives, Senators, TV stations, newspapers, etc., only four responded. One person, I spoke with over the phone with hopes that he will be able to help pass a bill in the House of Representatives that will benefit and protect our children from being bullied. The other three who reached out reside in another county in GA. However, they said they are willing to help and listen, however, I haven't heard from them since our conversation.

With hope, more people, parents, teachers, higher authorities, Representatives, Senators, Mayors, Governor, etc. will be willing to jump on board to save our babies live from the Silent Killer. Strength is in numbers; however, it only takes one person to make a difference and I am that one person who will give my all to STOP bullying!

The state of Georgia and others across the country need to pass a bill that all teachers, higher authorities, students, and parents need to be held accountable for their actions. Teachers and higher authorities who neglect to open their eyes to bullying need their licenses temporarily suspended or terminated. Their license should be treated like driver's licenses, with points deducted when not following the rules and regulations. Teachers and higher authorities' licenses should have points deducted when they do not follow the law that has been put in place against bullying. Teachers and everyone in the school system need to take anti-bullying courses yearly. They also need to take psychology courses yearly, such as childhood development, and Behavioral Inhibition in Children in order to work with students of different personalities.

Students who are bullies and parents of the bully should seek professional help, such as a 10 week through 52-week counseling session (depending on how severe the issue maybe) because something is going on inside the household.

Our children are killing themselves because of bullying, "The Silent Killer." Our children shouldn't have to suffer from the hands and voice of the Silent Killer. Our children's voices shouldn't go unheard because parents, students, teachers, higher authorities, and administrators do not care. Our sweet loving children should live a life of joy, love, peace, happiness, and laughter. They shouldn't know what stress is. They shouldn't be on medication because of what someone has done to them at school. We as parents shouldn't have to drag our children out of bed because they do not want to go to school. Our sweet babies who were once filled with so much life are being robbed of their birthright. How is that fair to our babies?

Something must be done. Something will be done.

Parents, guardians, students, teachers, and higher administrators need to be held accountable for their actions.

Our babies' lives matter. They deserve to live.

Introduction for the book:
Teachers Just Don't Understand: Bullying Hurts! 2nd edition

CHAPTER 1

THE FIRST-TIME I WAS BULLIED

I AM EMMANUEL. EMMANUEL Jackson. I am eleven years old and in the fifth grade. I am an outgoing and interesting person. I love skating, dancing, playing soccer, and spending time with my family. Unfortunately, going to school is a challenge for me—not because I am in speech therapy but because the same person has bullied me for three years. Every day is unpredictable. I never know what to expect. One might say, I am too young to experience bullying. Believe it or not, bullying happens to kids who are younger than me. When I am being bullied my teachers never listen. They always think I am making it up—or they will try to sugar-coat the situation. They fail to realize that children have feelings too, and we deserve to be heard. Teachers just don't understand. I know one day sooner or later things will be better, but I do not know when.

Since kindergarten people have always liked to pick on me and bully me. I never understood why. I am quiet and I try to stay to myself. I also try to treat people the way I want to be treated. I guess other people do not think the same as I do.

When I was in kindergarten, a boy named Karl always kicked me and said ugly things like, "You are ugly, your nose is too big, you are too short." So many negative things would come out of his mouth at least once or twice a week. I used to tell both of my teachers but the only thing they would do was talk to the student. We had to walk on a rug that looked like a ladder and talk about what happened. When it was the other person's turn to talk, we could move up a step. I asked myself, "why we are doing this? How is this going to help?" After we met at the top of the rug (which was supposed to be the top of the ladder) we had to apologize to each other. My teachers would think the problem was solved. It wasn't, because the same person would still pick on me, just more quietly, so the teacher wouldn't hear him. It only got worse, and more people began to pick on me because they knew they were not going to get into trouble. I was miserable going to school every day.

Each day when my mom picked me up from school, she would ask me how my day was. Most days, I would act as if everything was fine, and I would not tell her about my classmates bullying me. However, one day I had to say something because I was tired of hurting and being bullied so often.

I told my mom about how my classmates treated me. How they called me names, pushed and hit me. They often told me that I had a big head. My mom told me to say, "I know I have a big head. That's because I am smart!" I held my head down and said softly, "But Mom, that is not going to work. They are going to laugh at me."

I blurted out, "I tell my teachers but they never do anything! They would tell us to apologize. I do not understand, Mom, why do I have to apologize? After the other person apologizes, they hit me or call me names more quietly. Teachers just don't understand how I feel inside. They think since they asked us to apologize, their job is done. It isn't done, because I still hurt from the name-calling, hitting, humiliation, sleepless nights, and from feeling alone and depressed at school."

My mom looked at me in the rearview mirror. She had seen the tears forming in my eyes. My mom turned the car around and went back to the school. She was very upset. I was scared at first but my mom said, "Emmanuel, how long has this been going on?"

I replied, "Since the beginning of the school year." It was then February.

"Emmanuel, why is this the first time you are telling me this?" my mom asked.

"Mom, I did what you told me to do. I always tell my teachers, and I thought it was going to get better."

She said, "I asked you every day how was your day, and you always told me "fine." You have to tell me the truth, Emmanuel, so that I will know what is going on."

My mom parked the car. "Unbuckle your seatbelt. Come on," she said.

As we walked into the building my heart was racing. I was scared my teachers would be mad at me for telling my mom. My mom walked down to my classroom.

"Hello," Ms. Allen said with a smile.

My mother was not smiling. Ms. Allen's smile turned upside down and she said, "This looks serious. Is everything okay?"

My mom tried to stay calm, she said, "No, everything is not okay. Emmanuel was telling me about how his classmates make fun of him, call him names, put their hands on him, and it does not make him feel good. What is going on, and why is this happening? He said he told both you and Ms. Waters about it. He said the teachers use a rug that looks like a ladder to help solve their issues. Apparently, it's not working, because the situation is getting out of hand."

I was so afraid. I felt like I was telling on my teachers and getting them in trouble. My heart was beating so fast. I hid behind my mom and gripped hold of her leg.

Ms. Allen looked surprised as if it was the first time she'd heard about what was going on. My mom was waiting for answers. Ms. Allen asked my mother to take a seat, and my mom told me to sit down too.

I slowly took a seat but I was nervous, playing with my fingers.

Ms. Allen said, "Emmanuel what is going on?"

I looked at Ms. Allen with sadness in my eyes and said, "Karl called me horrible names. He would say I have a big butt, huge wide forehead, humongous nose. The list goes on and on."

I looked down at the table, fidgeting with my fingers, and said softly, "It doesn't make me feel good. His words hurt my feelings. It really hurts when everyone else laughs too. It is not a good feeling. Not a good feeling at all."

Ms. Allen said, "Emmanuel, how long has this been going on?"

I said, feeling embarrassed, "For a long time."

My mom looked Ms. Allen straight in the eye and said, "Emmanuel told me about what happened today."

Ms. Allen said, "Emmanuel and another student had a misunderstanding towards one another. Emmanuel thought the other student stepped on his foot. However, the other student said it was a mistake. I talked it out with Emmanuel and the student. I thought everything was okay, Emmanuel?"

I was breathing harder and harder because Karl always stepped on my foot on purpose. I was angry and said, "No! Karl knows exactly what he is doing! He makes it seem like it was a mistake to your face. Once we talk about it, he will laugh behind your back, shove his fist into his hand, and look at me as he bites his lip."

I continued and said, "He pushed me on the playground, kicked me and threw dirt in my face. I tried telling you about it, but you told me to get in line."

Ms. Allen said, "Emmanuel, I apologize. I had too much going on. I apologize. If something like this ever happens again, please let me know. I feel bad because I tell the students we will never know unless they tell us."

I cut off Ms. Allen and said, "I did tell you, I always tell you. Not all the time, because nothing is ever done so I stopped telling my teachers. If you're not around I will tell Ms. Waters, she too will ignore what I am saying."

I looked down at the table and said, "It is not fair to be treated this way."

My mom said, "Ms. Allen, I always tell Emmanuel to tell his teachers first. I also tell him I want him to come to me as well. I express to him over and over again to not hold anything in from me, because I want to help him and speak up for him when he feels nothing is being done."

My mom turned and looked at me and said, "Emmanuel, thank you for telling me because I cannot help you if you do not tell me."

I said softly, "Okay."

Ms. Allen said, "I am extremely sorry for not listening. I agree, Emmanuel. Come and tell me and please do not hold anything back, let me know. Ms. Jackson, I will address the other student and we will make sure this will not happen again."

My mom looked as if she did not believe my teacher, but she said, "Okay, but if this continues I will have no choice but to tell Emmanuel to defend himself. I will not allow my son to be bullied around. I will not tolerate it."

"I understand, but we do not want anyone to become violent," Ms. Allen replied.

My mother agreed, but she said, "Emmanuel is not going to sit here either and be a target. Hopefully, things will get better; if not, he will defend himself."

The next day, Karl, walked up to me, balled his fist and said, "Emmanuel the snitch."

I ignored him and walked to my desk. He walked behind me and pushed me. I had to catch my balance. I turned around and said, "Karl, don't put your hands on me."

He hit me again and said, "I just did. What are you going to do about it?"

I knew I had to defend myself because if I didn't, I was going to be a target for everyone to push around. I had had enough of Karl bullying me. I did not know my own strength, and I pushed him so hard he flipped over two desks and a chair.

I had never been in a fight before, and thought my heart was going to jump out of my chest. I was so scared, but I couldn't let Karl hit me and get away with it again. Enough was enough. I was ready to fight. Ms. Allen broke it up, sat us down, and talked to both of us.

I was proud of myself and I would do it again if I had to.

Introduction

THE CHOICES WE MAKE in life can make or break us. However, some people make choices out of selfish reasons; not knowing their actions at the present time will have repercussions in the future. We are told not to worry about tomorrow; for tomorrow is not promised. That could be very well true. However, what if tomorrow *is* promised; how would you reexamine yesterday? What would you do differently today? How would you prepare for tomorrow?

We are told to live for today, however, the question is—how many people live for "today?" If you are living for "today" at the end of the day, could you say you took care of all of your responsibilities? Each day has a purpose; each day creates a memory, and each day should be precious.

Ask yourself—did you put your best foot forward? Or did you point fingers at everyone else instead of focusing on what you need to improve? The important question is: at the end of each day are you satisfied with the decisions you've made?

Dear Fathers of the Fatherless Children:

Do you know your sons and daughters are AMAZING? They are full of life and they are truly a blessing. Your sons and daughters need you in their lives. How is it possible that at the beginning of the day when you open your eyes, your children are not on your priority list? Fathers of the fatherless children, your sons and daughters crave your presence and your support. They want you in their lives more than you will ever know. There isn't such a thing as a part-time father; your children shouldn't be treated as toys that you can throw in the closet when you are tired or when the going gets rough. Your sons and daughters are human; they should feel loved and nothing less at all times. You say you love your children, but actions speak louder than words; stand up and be a father to your sons and daughters.

Fathers of the fatherless children, open your eyes and know your presence is very critical. Be your son's hero and let him know he can conquer the world. Be your daughter's first knight in shining armor. Be a part of your son's and daughter's success instead of their pain.

Introduction for the book:
A Woman's Love Is Never Good Enough 2nd Edition

Love.

What is love? It is the essence of the unknown and will overwhelm you if you do not realize you are giving too much of yourself.

Love is an intense emotion that will take a toll on you mentally, emotionally, and physically in an unselfish, yet bittersweet way that develops into a deep affection; and sometimes, an unknown outcome.

Love is filled with a lot of sacrifices and resentment and is underestimated in so many ways. It is something of a Catch-22 and an overwhelming source of empowerment. You might feel as though love didn't give you an answer to the questions that you asked. You've been waiting for days, even years; and perhaps you will never receive an answer at all. Maybe you've received an answer; however, it wasn't what you expected. The question is—did you accept the answer, or are you still searching for the answer you desire?

Love is a strange word. It can be misleading and confusing. It can break you down with tender grace and mercy, while at the same time building you up to become a powerful force—and after that, you will never be the same.

The ripple effects of love are beautiful and peaceful, yet can also be disturbing and ruthless. At times, love takes advantage of its powers; it causes you to suffer from loving someone too much and finding yourself lost, without hope and giving too much of yourself to the point that you suffer because you're neglecting yourself. It can cause you to lose faith. Its tremendous effect has a full impact as you find peace and happiness in your life.

Love will open your eyes to realize you are not the victim; instead, you are victorious over the trials, battles, and challenges of life.

Love will show you that you do not have to search for it because it abides in you whole-heartedly. Love can be bittersweet but its grace is patience. Love is difficult but its mercy is tender. At times love might make you feel empty but you are never alone.

Love abounds against all odds. One thing about love is that it comes with many sacrifices. Its good intentions always reassure you that in order to love someone else, you must be willing to love yourself first.

ABOUT THE AUTHOR

Charlena E. Jackson, B.S., M.S., M.H.A. is a professor at a university in Georgia. She is a prolific writer and has published several books, among them being: No Cross, No Crown: Trust God Through the Battle (1st & 2nd edition), Teachers Just Don't Understand Bullying Hurts (1st & 2nd edition), I'm Speaking Up but You're Not Listening (1st & 2nd edition), A Woman's Love is Never Good Enough (1st & 2nd edition), Dear Fathers of the Fatherless Children, Dying on the Inside and Suffocating on the Outside, and Unapologetic for My Flaws and All (1st and 2nd edition). Her positive, dedicated, and determined attitude has encouraged many people to put up a good fight for justice and to be treated with respect. She is currently working on her Ph.D. in Healthcare Administration. Charlena is a much-loved inspirational speaker. She loves to read, roller skate, cycle, write, and travel. Charlenaejackson@gmail.com

Article
Why have suicides among black youths skyrocketed?
https://www.ajc.com/lifestyles/health/why-have-suicides-among-black-youths-skyrocketed/94zwzXWHeeIBfmncYWRK6N/#

www.ingramcontent.com/pod-product-compliance
Lightning Source LLC
Chambersburg PA
CBHW022338280326
41934CB00006B/680